SYLVIA SIDNEY

Question and Answer Book on Needlepoint

Baby zebra; see chapter 3, project 1

SYLVIA SIDNEY
Question and Answer Book on Needlepoint

VNR VAN NOSTRAND REINHOLD COMPANY
New York Cincinnati Toronto London Melbourne

Also by the author:
Sylvia Sidney Needlepoint Book

Van Nostrand Reinhold Company
Regional Offices:
New York Cincinnati Chicago Millbrae Dallas
Van Nostrand Reinhold Company
International Offices:
London Toronto Melbourne

Designed by Rosa Delia Vasquez

Published by Van Nostrand Reinhold Company
A Division of Litton Educational Publishing, Inc.
450 West 33rd Street, New York, N.Y. 10001

16 15 14 13 12 11 10 9 8 7 6 5 4 3 2 1

Library of Congress Cataloging in Publication Data

Sidney, Sylvia.
    Question and answer book on needlepoint.

    Bibliography: p.
    1. Canvas embroidery. I. Title.
TT778.C3S5   746.4'4   74-5949
ISBN 0-442-27882-9

Every experience deeply felt in life needs to be passed along—whether it be through words or music, chiseled in stone, painted with a brush or sewn with a needle—it is a way of reaching for immortality.
—Thomas Jefferson

Contents

Introduction: Why Another Book on Needlepoint?

Why another book on needlepoint? I have asked myself that question many times since the publication of my first book in 1968. Then, there were only a few books devoted entirely to needlepoint, and even the general books on stitchery dealt with needlepoint in a perfunctory manner.

But enter a bookstore today, go to the hobby or crafts section, and you will find an entire shelf filled with books on needlepoint —and two more shelves filled with needlecraft and embroidery books that have elevated the formerly neglected needlepoint chapter to star status. So why another book on needlepoint?

I look out of my window here in the country, watching a spectacular sunset, and I remember the time I was playing in Neil Simon's *Barefoot in the Park* on Broadway. There had been several exhibitions of my needlepoint pieces, and they were being sold at high prices—I could hardly believe how much people were paying for them. My pieces were considered collector's items. Fashion columnist Eugenia Sheppard did an interview with me on my needlepoint, which appeared in the old *New York Herald-Tribune*. A few days later I got a telephone call from Van Nostrand Reinhold Company. They wanted to pay me money—actual, real money—to write a book on needlepoint. I couldn't believe that either! A book had never entered my mind!

That book did a marvelous thing for me—it bridged generations. For example, a few years ago, when I needed some alterations on dresses and skirts, I went to see a young seamstress in a neighboring town. She was delighted to meet me. At dinner that night, I learned later, she had announced to her parents, "Guess who came to see *me* today? Sylvia Sidney." Amazed, her father asked, "The movie star?" "No," she replied, "the lady who wrote that marvelous book on needlepoint." She really didn't know I had ever made movies, she only knew of me because of the book. Bless her!

A year or so later I met a young woman at the home of a friend of mine. She was a recent Farmington School graduate, and a needlepointer. She admired the work in my pieces in my friend's home and bombarded me with questions about stitches, designing, marking canvases, blocking, etc. Later, I learned she skimmed through her mother's copy of my book. At one point she looked up almost thunderstruck and asked her parents, "She's an actress, too?"

That first book brought me an entirely new public. Through their questions I learned a lot more about needlepoint, but the biggest question of all went unanswered. How is it possible, with the plethora of needlepoint books in the stores, that the same questions are asked of me time and time again? What is it that my book, and all the others, failed to communicate, so that men and women all over the country still have questions left unanswered? Where did I, and the other needlepoint authors, miss?

For the last few years, among my other activities, I have made countless appearances lecturing on needlepoint, and promoting the book and a line of commercial kits that I designed. Aside from acting appearances on tour with plays, in dinner theatres, in summer and winter stock, I did eight solid weeks of appearances in more than forty department stores across the country. The most exciting time for me in all the lectures was the question-and-answer period. It was then that I found out what it was that people really wanted to know.

My schedule during that eight-week period of touring department stores might interest you. One just doesn't suddenly appear, as if born that way, in full make-up, false eyelashes, pressed suit, hair in place, with all the props in order, notes, slides, projector, etc., without an enormous amount of planning, organization, and help.

The daily schedule as a general rule was something like this:

8 a.m.—Television studio for that particular city's local *Today* show.

9:30 a.m.—Press breakfast, interviews, and photographs.

11 a.m. to 12:30 p.m.—Store, art-needlework or book department, 45-minute lecture with slides and question-and-answer period.

1 p.m.—Lunch with store executives and more press.

2:30 to 4 p.m.—Back to the floor.

5 to 6 p.m.—Back to the hotel to change, pack, feed my dog, and rush to the airport to catch the plane to the next city.

Sometimes the programmed logistics of transportation planning was peculiar to the extreme. One time I was about 100 miles between cities. It took one hour to get to the airport from the hotel I was leaving. The plane was late. It finally landed in a near-historic thunderstorm. We boarded, and after much bouncing and tossing about, it begain to rain—in the plane! Fortunately there were plenty of newspapers on board, and we passed them to each other. We sat crowded together, bouncing up and down and holding the sodden newspapers over our heads.

In driving rain and lightning, we finally landed. There were the people from the department store, the buyer and the public-relations staff, to greet me with dozens of gorgeous roses. Imagine their dismay to see me—wet head, wrinkled suit and face—rushing through the airport yelling, "It rained *in* the plane! I've got to find my dog. He didn't have a newspaper to put over his head!"

Finally I arrived at the hotel, too late for room service, too late for the dining room, too late for anything. Famished, I settled for a soggy, overdone cheeseburger and some limp French fries from a nearby drugstore.

More than five hours to travel one hundred miles! My belated apologies to all those patient buyers and overworked public-relations people who had the experience of greeting me on such disastrous occasions, when my teeth would be set on edge just by the sound of my own voice.

The next day? See schedule above!

Sometimes I was lucky. I would remain in a city for two days to make appearances the second day in outlying branch stores. Marshall Field & Company in Chicago was a good example of this. I spent the first day in the downtown store and the second day visiting two branch stores. The Marshall Field people did a particularly good job. The first day a crowd of more than 1,500 people jammed the art-needlework department. They got the crowd because their promotion and publicity was so good. Everything ran like clockwork. It was a joy. Two other stores that did particularly good jobs were Rich's in Atlanta and Frederick & Nelson in Seattle.

That eight-week tour was exhausting but most instructive for me. After designing kits, touring in *Come Blow Your Horn, Cabaret, Barefoot in the Park, Butterflies Are Free, Suddenly Last Summer,* and *Arsenic and Old Lace,* radio and television appearances, a television movie, the movie *Summer Wishes, Winter Dreams,* two eye operations (more about that later) and television commercials, it took conducting a seminar for a large corporation to make me see the light—a tiny glimmer, but light. That did it!

11

My pug dogs, who always travel with me, are under the table at my feet. The needlepoint butterfly is shown in color on page 78.

The seminar was attended by a group of people who should have had practically no questions to ask of me. In fact, they should have been able to give me instruction, and fill me in on a few things. But there I stood being asked the *very same questions* by top buyers, instructors, and needlecraft specialists that I had heard throughout the entire department store tour and heard from the young Farmington graduate—and *in the same order!*

In spite of my book, and all the other books on needlepoint jamming the shelves and counters in book stores across the country, the needs of the beginner and the advanced needle-pointer apparently were not being satisfied. So this time around I will try to answer those questions clearly and simply, those questions asked me at the lectures I have given. I have saved all those questions scribbled on memo sheets and index cards and passed up to me on lecture platforms. Some of the lectures were taped, and I have all the questions I have been asked in letters. These questions fall into several large groups and will be answered in the following chapters of this book.

I have also designed several projects just for this book, which I will discuss and explain from binding the edges of the cut canvas right through completion and blocking. And I'll show you the versatility and flexibility of our hobby and diversion—needlepoint.

As I sit here now, watching the sun recede, I am reminded of my favorite mother-in-law, a beautiful, wise, and most knowledgeable woman. When asked how one went about beginning to write a play or a book, she advised, "The most important gift a writer needs is the ability to apply a certain portion of the anatomy to the seat of a chair and have it remain there for long periods of time. When a writer is standing or pacing or staring out of a window, he is *not* writing!"

It's exactly that way with me. I have difficulty sitting for long periods of time. I procrastinate, I stare at the blank sheet of paper in my typewriter. I stare out of the window. But for me, it's the first step, whether starting a new piece of needlepoint, learning a new part for a play, or washing my hair.

12

1
How Do You Design Needlepoint?

Before replying to questions for this book, I thought a great deal about the answers myself. Words are wonderful, yet dangerous, because they have so many different meanings and nuances for different people. For instance, in the theatre you often hear of actors discussing the "design" of a performance or a character. But that's another keg of nails, and I don't intend to write a book about *that!* So before there is total confusion, let's get our definitions clearly defined.

I lifted my old heavy *Oxford Universal Dictionary* from the shelf:

"design: a plan or scheme conceived in the mind of something to be done."

"pattern: an example or model deserving of imitation."

Then I thought, perhaps we ought to be a little more up to date. So I lifted the new heavy *Random House American Dictionary* off the floor:

"design: to prepare the preliminary sketch or plan for work to be executed, to plan or fashion artistically or skillfully."

"pattern: a decorative design for china, wallpaper, fabrics, etc."

Now those definitions don't sound too awesome, do they? Personally, I prefer the *Oxford* definitions, because they seem a little less pretentious and confusing. I have learned that the moment you use such words as "artistic," "artistically," or "artist" it has the sound of something beyond us poor mortals. Believe me, if this poor mortal can do it, it is possible, with the will and the wish, for you to learn what I have learned and to learn from the mistakes I have made.

And now that we have reliable definitions as our standards, hopefully you will understand what I am trying to communicate to you.

Questions and Answers

I have picked the following questions, hit or miss, from the hundreds that I have been asked about designing needlepoint. Some of the questions on designing overlap into other areas, which I will save for later chapters. But generally, they are very much in the same vein.

1. Do you design your own patterns?

2. Is it advisable to take design lessons to do good needlework?

1. All the pieces I have executed in the last 15 or 20 years I have designed myself.

2. I am not quite sure what "design lessons" would be, but I believe that any kind of schooling or training is not wasteful, and can be rewarding and useful in many ways. Design is often included in art courses, although I don't feel it is necessary to be an artist to create good designs for needlepoint. See the remarks later (page 16) about transferring designs.

3. Did you study painting?

3. No, I did not study painting. I am a self-taught Sunday painter, and in my estimation, not a very good one. Perhaps needlepoint serves me as an outlet in that small frustration. The only real training and schooling I ever had was to be an actress. This may have been fortunate for me, when you consider that over the years, I have worked with such brilliant and talented designers as Boris Aaronson, Travis Banton, Alvin Colt, Eldon Elder, Edith Head, Don Loper, Noel Taylor, Michael Woulfe and scores of unknown and unsung talented theatrical designers, heroes, and heroines who lived through my crankiness, nerves, and panic. Some of their knowledge and taste surely must have influenced me and rubbed off on me.

4. Do you plan your designs from a painter's viewpoint or that of a needlepoint artist?

5. Do you spend as much time planning a design as executing it?

4. Although I paint all my designs on paper first, I have to plan and think in terms of needlepoint because the medium, materials, and effects are very different from a painter's.

5. This is where the road separates. A painter will spend months, sometimes years on a painting. Planning and designing for needlepoint never take as long as the actual execution.

14

6. I have seen some beautiful antique pieces of furniture combined with what could be considered modern design in needlepoint. That is a matter of personal taste. At times I prefer to stick to the traditional, but decor is becoming much less rigid. Today there is more freedom in the mixing of periods and styles. The word being used all over the place *now* is "eclectic." Look that up in *your* dictionary! That's what very elegant people call my house. I call it *circa* VESLO (very expensive storage left overs)!

6. Does the design of a chair have to be considered in selecting the design for a needlepoint seat?

7. I wouldn't dream of *graphing myself!* In fact, looking at myself in the mirror is getting to be more and more of a gamble. I think I know what the questioner meant. Yes, I use graph paper, because I have lots of it around the house. I have found that I confine myself less and less to the rigidity of the squares of the graph paper. Then, too, graph paper doesn't always line up exactly with the various canvases, and that can be extremely confusing. More and more I work from the actual painting or drawing itself, and decide as I stitch and progress how to make the shading imitate the painting. More about this in Chapter 5, question 10.

7. Do you graph yourself before needlepoint?

Designing Needlepoint

To me, designing needlepoint is very personal. Some pieces I have done, I feel, really accomplished what I originally set out to do, and there are others that haven't. But at least I tried to do the best I knew how at the time.

This chapter on design is specifically addressed to all you needlepointers who want to start from scratch and do your own thing. For those of you who prefer to buy kits, painted canvases, or partially worked designs, this chapter might make you a little more daring.

There are so many ways to come by designs. But first, you must have the desire to want to adapt a design. Then you must ask yourself some questions: What do you want it to look like? What is its purpose? Who or what is it for?

Sources for ideas are endless—wallpapers, china, flower prints, old rugs, seed catalogues, printed fabrics, the texture in woven material, art books, graphics magazines, even doodles. And it's not stealing, consciously or unconsciously. By the time you have planned and adapted your "theft," the work will be totally yours.

I think if we travel together from the beginning of my journeys with some of the recent pieces I have made, it will clarify for you how I travel from idea, to design, to plan, to corrections, elimination, and finally to the finish line.

Why not start with a couple of tough ones first. I say they are tough, because you must count so carefully, and a simple mistake can be costly in time and energy. Tears won't help, believe me.

These first two "tough ones" both involve lettering of quotations. Lettering in needlepoint is very easy to execute but difficult to plan. The letters must line up evenly and be evenly spaced. One very important thing to remember (and this is where graph paper can throw you off sometimes if you are not careful): Minimum height for letters must be five rows or meshes; minimum width three rows; minimum space between letters one row; and at least two or three rows between words (both horizontally and vertically). The spacing between the lines is a matter of choice and balance, depending on the number of words and how large the finished piece will eventually be.

16

Count your letters and spaces for each line and work from the center out, to the left and to the right. This will give you a clear idea of what kind of margins you have, and where you will have to make some compromises with some of the lettering. All this should be done on paper before you even touch the canvas. If you are using graph paper, the holes must be just as large as the meshes on the canvas; otherwise when you transfer the marks to the canvas you may come out with fewer rows than you intended.

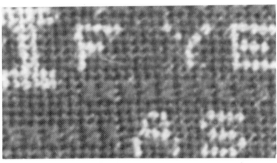

Spacing of letters or numbers must be carefully worked out so they will have clarity and not crowd each other. My rules are: A minimum height of 5 meshes and a minimum width of 3 meshes for each letter; minimum space between letters of 1 mesh; minimum space between words of 2 meshes; and minimum space between lines of lettering 3 meshes.

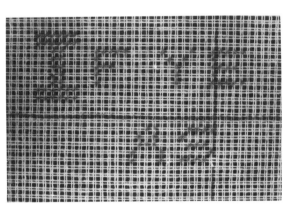

This is the same area marked on the canvas before stitching. Graph paper can only be used as a guide. It is impossible to trace lettering, and it must be counted out on the canvas.

If you plan your lettering on graph paper you can count the boxes to help you mark the canvas. However, it can be confusing if the graph paper boxes are not exactly the same size as the meshes in the canvas.

17

Project 1 (page 19)

For years I have wanted to do the parable of the mustard seed from the Bible. I found my own Bible too modern and unpoetic. I sought the help of dear friends who live quite near me, the James Douglases (he's the well-known television actor). Dawn Douglas is a lovely lady and very giving—in this matter, a little too giving. I received from her one day a very heavy envelope with four references from Matthew and Luke from the King James version and three from the new Confraternity version of the Bible.

Well, I was confused. The one I liked best and the one closest to what I thought of as the parable of the mustard seed was from the King James version, Matthew 17:20. It reads:

If ye have faith as a grain of mustard seed, ye shall say unto this moutain, Remove hence to yonder place; and it shall remove; and nothing shall be impossible to you.

But there were too many words. How could I confine it to the simple idea, the essence of its meaning? After much thought and with no intention to offend, but with reverence, I decided to edit it. My edited parable reads, "If ye have faith as a grain of mustard seed nothing shall be impossible to you." Actually, this, I think, is what I remember hearing when I was very young.

The first drawings I made were with very Gothic and fancy lettering. I wanted the piece to be only 9 by 18 inches (easy for framing), and I wanted it on 10-point penelope canvas (10 double meshes per inch). Types of canvas are discussed in Chapter 2. It wouldn't work. It looked too busy and *fussy*. Back to the drawing board, and more graph paper.

This time I went completely in the other direction. I planned very simple block lettering. Although it looked very cold and hard, I knew it would work better for the size of the piece and the canvas.

Now I had to figure out something to give it softness. I thought I would give it a delicate border of mustard seed flowers but decided that would look rigid and *cute*. I also realized I had no idea of what a mustard seed flower looked like. I went through all my books on gardening, spices and herbs, and all my seed catalogues. I found only one small picture, badly out of focus and so poorly printed it was useless.

18

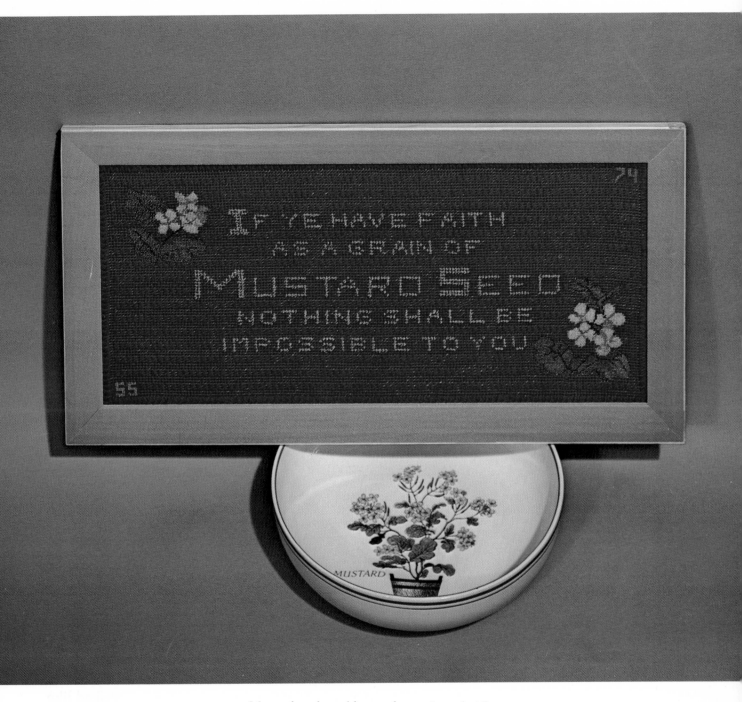

Mustard seed parable; see chapter 1, project 1

I had almost given up hope of ever getting my mustard seed off the ground, certainly not out of it! One day, still steaming with frustration, I decided I had better get cracking with my Christmas shopping (more frustration). I was in The Square Peg, a beautiful, smart shop in the next town, Woodbury, run by Marin Shealy, a marvelous gal. Just the month before, she had run and been elected first selectman, a New England equivalent of mayor. She is the *first* first select*woman* in the history of the town, and doing a fantastic job.

There it was. A bowl (which I needed like another hole in my head) with a delicately and beautifully done painting of a mustard plant in full flower with clearly defined leaves. My Christmas list fell to the floor, I grabbed the bowl and pushed my way through the crowded store angering quite a number of customers and calling out, "Put this on my bill."

I raced home, barely observing speed limits and stop signs, ran upstairs to my workroom, and did some quick drawings of the painting in the bottom of the bowl. Once again, they were much too busy. I reached for my scissors and did some cut-outs of the drawings, separating parts of them into small sprays and placing them around the graph paper with the lettering on it.

Finally I got what I thought was the right composition or design. It was not four sprays, one in each corner. That, again, was too busy, or so it seemed to me. I chose instead two sprays in diagonally opposite corners, and pointed in different directions. It was just the answer to soften the boldness of the lettering.

I had already decided that the background was to be a soft, almost claret red and the letters in a golden mustard color. The letters and background for the letters were to be done in tent stitch. But the more I worked on the piece, the harsher the mustard-colored wool seemed against the red background, so I toned it down by re-embroidering over the letters with a soft mustard silk floss. I would have done something like this in any case, because it gives the letters a raised effect. I completed the rest of the background by alternating two rows of tent stitch with one row of straight cashmere stitch, which is simply an elongated mosaic stitch. I have never quite understood the names some stitches are called.

The flowers and leaves were just too small and delicate to look good on a 10-point penelope canvas. So I split the doubled threads of the canvas, making four stitches for every one mesh or 20 stitches to the linear inch instead of 10. I gave the whole piece a border of two-step herringbone to frame it and give a change of texture at the edge.

20

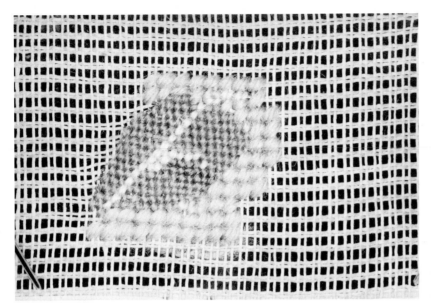

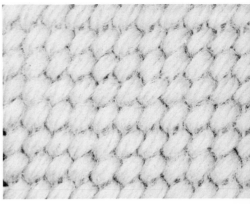

Tent stitch. Step-by-step directions for the stitches mentioned in the book begin on page 99. See page 99 for tent-stitch directions.

Penelope (duo) canvas worked over split and unsplit double threads. Notice how two different sizes of stitches can be worked on the same canvas in this way. The half-cross stitch pictured here is discussed in Chapter 2.

Straight cashmere stitch. See page 100 for directions.

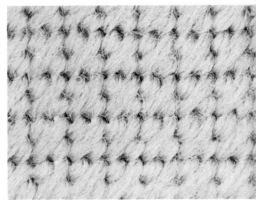

Two-step herringbone stitch. From this basic stitch, many variations can be created. Three-step, four-step, five-step, and six-step herringbone are developed from it. See page 102 for directions.

Horizontal mosaic stitch. See page 101 for directions.

Opposite
My pillow; see chapter 1, project 3

Two bargello pillows; see chapter 1,
project 4

Tobacco pillow; see chapter 1, project 2

Project 2 (page 22)

For a very dear, chain-smoking friend—no, a carton-smoking friend—I thought I could hint my disapproval by needlepointing this little poem, which has been attributed to Robert Burns:

Tobacco is a filthy weed,
From the devil doth proceed,
Robs your pocket,
Burns your clothes,
Makes a chimney of your nose.

Also his birthday was approaching, and he was moving into a gorgeous new house. I wanted a massive masculine look, because I could already see it on a perfectly beautiful red-leather antique settee he had just bought in England.

I was on tour with Neil Simon's *Come Blow Your Horn* at the time. When I'm out with a show I always travel with one small trunk that is the bane of the lives of company managers, truckers, and stage crews. It's my needlepoint trunk, and it contains wools, silks, canvas, paints, drawing materials, needles, and graph paper. As far as I am concerned, whenever we move from one city to the next *that* trunk and my dog crates have to be accounted for first of all. The scenery, props, costumes, and all the paraphernalia and trappings it takes to get the show on the road are no concern of mine!

I wanted the tobacco piece to be a very heavy rap on the knuckles to a very, very heavy smoker. It must have been on a Sunday night off between cities that I holed in at some hotel and started planning the design. Once again I faced the problem of sources. I had some pictures of tobacco leaves I had found in an advertisement for you can guess what. Should I do the background with leaves scattered around? Okay, but where would I put the poem?

Although I wanted to rap those knuckles, I wanted the message to be subtle and the pillow decorative. That's what made me decide to do one large tobacco leaf with lettering going into and through it. I had a large piece of 12-point penelope canvas that I thought would serve. I didn't want to do it on 10-point canvas because that would have made it enormous, and a smaller gauge would have taken too long to execute. See page 36 for a further discussion of canvas gauges.

When I finally worked out the letters and finished painting the leaf, the piece would be about 18 by 20 inches in size. That was a lot of canvas to cover in the short time I had. The lettering is not as rigid as on the mustard seed parable, and the spacing is freer because of the rhyme. I went a little wild with the capitals, but that's what attracts the eye, and makes the viewer read the rest of the line.

I chose red for the letters because of the red settee, and split the canvas threads (see page 20). The tobacco leaf is done in tones of mixed shades of rust, gold, brown, and a very soft orange. In the original sketch I had a burning cigarette in the left-hand corner. It seemed right at the time to have it balance the heaviness of the large tobacco leaf. Two things decided me against the cigarette. One, while waiting in an airport, I accidentally burned a hole in the canvas with my own cigarette —the old knuckle-rapper herself! The second thing was that the cigarette really looked awful. Some members of the company thought I should leave the burn hole unworked. Under no circumstances was I going to start all over again.

Time was getting short. It was easy to readjust the plan, eliminate the burning cigarette, patch the burn hole (how to repair canvas will be covered in Chapter 5), and do a massive border that would completely frame the poem.

I chose three shades of soft beige so I wouldn't be taking a risk. Those shades would blend with whatever he chose for the rest of the room and would stand out very well on the red-leather settee. The leaf and background for the poem were done in tent stitch (see page 21).

Then I started the border with seven rows of knotted stitch done over five meshes. The knotted stitch is really a slight variation of the slanting Gobelin stitch, which works very quickly and has a beautiful texture and movement. To the untrained eye, it looks very complicated, yet it covers canvas with great speed. I put Scotch stitch in the four corners and at the centers of the four sides to break up the monotonous look. Finally I pulled all the colors together by finishing the border with four rows of six-step herringbone stitch.

The pillow was finished in time for the birthday. It is now five years later. My dear friend is still smoking like a fiend, and I am still burning holes in things with my own cigarette. But the tobacco leaf pillow looks gorgeous on that red-leather settee.

Wildflower ottoman; see chapter 2, project 1

Footstool with pineapple design; see chapter 2, project 2

Pillow with pineapple design; see chapter 2, project 3

Knotted stitch. See page 104 for directions.

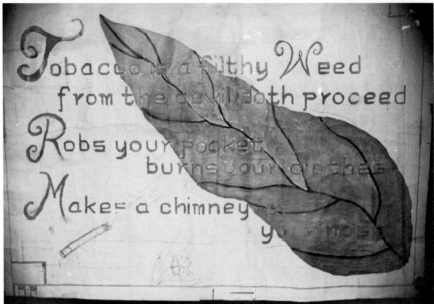

Original sketch for the tobacco leaf piece. It was later changed to leave out the burning cigarette.

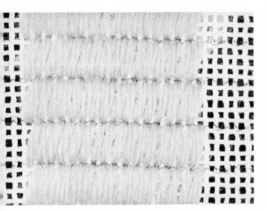

Slanting Gobelin stitch. See page 105 for directions.

Six-step herringbone stitch. See page 107 for directions.

Scotch stitch. See page 105 for directions.

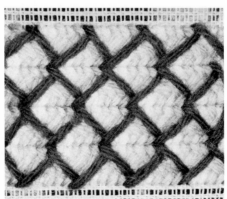

Six-step herringbone 2.

Project 3 (page 23)

This one is sort of a bonus and fun to do. It also illustrates how easily a "design" can evolve without drawing or painting or even much planning. This is *my* pillow—one of the very few things I have done that *I* own. I don't know what prompted me to do it; it was partly as an experiment, I guess, and partly that I cannot stand waste in any way, shape, or form. I had on hand all those odds and ends of wool that every needle worker has left over from all the pieces I had done.

The most planning that is necessary is the drawing of four lines on your canvas. Simply divide the canvas in half, draw a horizontal line at the half-way point, and then a vertical line. You now have a cross, which divides your canvas into four equal sections. Where the lines meet at the exact center, draw diagonally from corner to corner.

From the center out, follow the diagonal lines using the diagonal mosaic stitch (see page 54). This works as a guide for the rest of the piece. Then work around the canvas with horizontal mosaic from the center out.

The color combinations are endless, particularly if you put three or four different shades of yarn in your needle at once. Doing this makes a beautiful blend. And what a good feeling to know that you are using up all that wool that you've long ago lost the dye lot numbers for or for which the dye lots no longer even exist. The pillow measures 14 by 14 inches and is done on 5-point penelope rug canvas.

When the pillow was completed, I still had enough yarn left over in the colors I had used to make a fringe to go all around the edge. Fringing is well worth the little extra time it takes to do. Fringe not only makes the pillow look larger but adds a nice finishing touch.

Fringe. See page 113 for directions.

29

Project 4 (page 23)

This is a good example of how different the same design can appear by simply changing the shading and rebalancing the yarn colors. I cannot in all honesty say that this is my own original design. It is a very traditional bargello motif. I have seen it in museums on chairs, pillows, footstools, and countless other things.

It is well near impossible to trace the true, factual origin of bargello, which today is one of the most popular forms of needlepoint. In 14th-century Florence, there was a political prison called the Bargello, occupying an unused palace built more than a century before. Probably the name of the prison and the name of this particular style of stitchery have no connection. It seems highly unlikely to me that bargello as we know it today originated in the dank, dark lower-depth dungeons of the prison with a bunch of political prisoners sitting around doing stitchery to pass the time of day.

In the 19th century the old prison was converted into the National Museum of Florence, where some of the chairs in the collections have seat covers that are excellent examples of bargello. Even here, there can hardly be a connection, since bargello flourished in the 14th and 15th centuries in all the royal courts of Europe. So the origin of bargello—myth or legend—remains a mystery to us.

Getting back to this project, once you have decided on the main theme or movement of your bargello stitchery, you can let your own color combinations and your imagination fly. These two pieces are on 16-point mono canvas. In fact, I worked both designs on one piece of canvas, so I really only had to count and mark it once.

I have a pair of long, narrow mustardy-color velvet pillows, and I thought I could sew the two pieces right onto the pillows (more of that in a later chapter).

The stitchery was the simple bargello stitch—four meshes straight up and two meshes down, one mesh over. I took three-ply yarn and split it, using only two strands in the needle. Once you begin this particular type of bargello, you can hardly stop. It's worse than a bowl of salted nuts within arm's reach. And it goes so quickly, even with a fine canvas. I did both pieces during backstage waits in *Barefoot in the Park*, in five weeks!

30

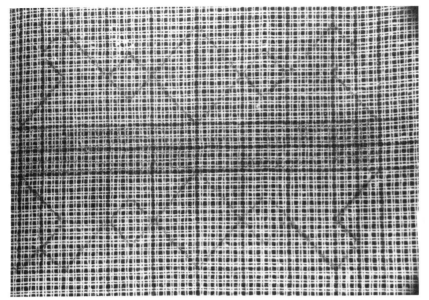

Variations of bargello markings. For any design like this, first mark canvas in halves, horizontally and vertically, then in halves again diagonally. The canvas is slightly darkened through the center area to show that by counting and marking only once, you can have two marked designs, if you cut the canvas apart through the center area.

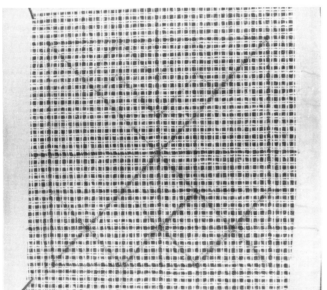

Marked canvas for bargello pillows. The top and bottom of this design are derived from the same beginning divisions of the canvas, horizontally, vertically, and diagonally, but are then varied slightly.

Bargello stitch. Insert needle 4 meshes above where it comes to the front, and bring it out 2 meshes below and 1 mesh to right or left from where it was inserted, depending on whether you are going up or down. Once the first row of stitches has been established, it is very easy to follow the pattern for the other rows. "Bargello", "flame", and "Florentine" embroidery are basically the same and are derived from the straight Gobelin stitch (see Chapter 4) or old satin stitch.

Project 5

Now this is really a true story of how a "design" is designed. I went to the west coast a couple of years ago to do a television movie, *Do Not Spindle, Fold or Mutilate*, starring Helen Hayes, Myrna Loy, and Mildred Natwick.

In many ways, for me, it was more than a job. First of all, that great lady, Helen Hayes, was playing the leading role. This particular meeting for both of us was emotional and nostalgic when she walked into the rehearsal hall. So very much had happened to both of us since the first time we met. If it had not been for this lady, it is quite possible that I might never have become an actress.

In the spring of 1926 she had made one of the most fantastic personal hits on Broadway in James Barrie's *What Every Woman Knows*. She was not only my idol, but the idol of almost every aspiring young actress at the time. She personally gave me much encouragement and inspiration. In 1926, the ten-year difference in our ages was, to me, enormous. But ten year's difference when you are circling 60 and 70 (Miss Hayes, I don't believe, was ever coy about her age) matters very little, if at all.

Myrna and I had been friends for a long time. As a matter of fact, she was literally responsible for my getting that part. I barely knew Mildred Natwick. All along I thought she was the youngest of the four. But I just looked it up. She is older than I am by two years. Although she created the part of the mother in Neil Simon's *Barefoot in the Park*, she, Myrna, and myself, among many others, have to thank Mr. Simon's genius for many, many months of work playing that part—and paying my bills. I don't know Myrna's age, and I wouldn't dream of asking.

That's quite a build-up, I suppose, to explain the evolvement of a needlepoint design, but I think you should know some of the background. One day when all four of us were having lunch, Miss Hayes (my respect for her makes it still difficult for me to even type the name Helen) asked me about designing a piece of needlepoint for her to do. She is an avid needlepointer. She had read and studied my book and loved it. How about that? And from my former idol!

Now, after all those years, I could finally help her. For her daughter-in-law she wanted to do a framed piece called, "A Mother-in-Law's Prayer." It reads:

Oh, Lord, help me not to be helpful.

32

Since I knew when I went to the west coast I would only be there three or four weeks, I didn't have my "supply trunk" with me. So I thought it was impossible for me to design this for her. The next morning she arrived at the studio with my book in hand. And she was very definite about how she wanted the piece to look and how large it should be when framed.

"It will be easy," she said. On page 80 she found the style of lettering she wanted. On page 63 she found the border and the background brick stitch she wanted, so she could do it quickly.

The next time, when she and I weren't needed for a scene, we went to a great shop in Beverly Hills. She gave them her specifications and the color of yarns she wanted. As I remember, they were pale blues and pinks. By the time we had finished the movie, the canvas was ready for her, and Miss Hayes was set to go. Now, in every sense, as far as I am concerned, Miss Helen Hayes designed that piece!

Succeeding chapters are involved with other questions, and answers. But please, don't despair, because there is hardly any area of the craft that does not involve design in some way. I still really prefer to call it "planning."

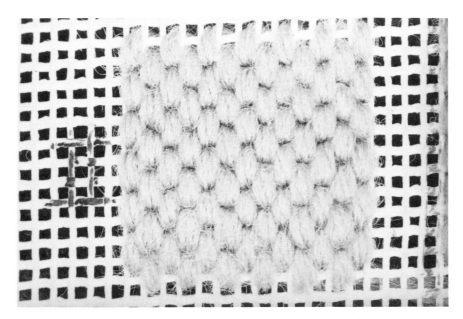

Brick stitch. See directions on page 115.

33

2
What Is the Best Canvas, and How Do You Mark It?

What is the best canvas? As to the matter of quality, there is not much choice. Linen canvas is very difficult to find these days. In fact, it is practically non-existent. But linen canvas is absolutely the best.

Most canvas today is cotton. That in itself is not a deterrent to its usefulness, nor does it imply a lack of quality. A few words of caution, however: Look for canvas that is woven in good clear square meshes with good sizing, not too stiff or too soft.

I've been told that good sizing has a fine glaze, but I've never noticed that. I judge the sizing by simply feeling it. As I have said, if it lacks sizing, it will be soft and won't hold its shape while you are working on it. Then, too, there is the danger that inadequately sized threads may be very strained while the stitches are worked, and could break in blocking.

If there is too much sizing, the canvas will feel harsh to the fingertips and will be too abrasive on the wool or silk as you work. In other words, your yarn will fray very quickly.

If you work on a piece for a very long time, and carry it around a lot and fold it, the canvas is apt to soften and become mushy. The stiffness can be restored easily and the square meshes lined up again by pressing lightly with a steam iron on the reverse side. Or you can spray it with aerosol starch on the back and go over it with a warm iron. The squareness of the meshes will be restored, and you can continue with your work as though the canvas were brand new.

Another word of caution: Be wary of the so-called canvases that are made of plastic or some other *ersatz* material. Some of them are like cardboard. It is quite obvious that there will be no blocking necessary. It does indeed retain its shape, but how the devil can work done on it ever be made into a pillow? Coasters, maybe! Then there is another kind (no names, please). It is some kind of plastic or polyester. It does soften and get out of shape, but I imagine blocking would be practically impossible. So let's stick to the good, old-fashioned, well-known canvases. They last forever. Just go to a museum and see for yourself!

34

There are two kinds of canvas—mono and penelope. Mono canvas obviously explains itself. It is a single thread woven horizontally crossing a single thread vertically.

Now penelope. . . . I have often wondered why it is called that. Could it have been named after Penelope, wife of Ulysses? She, the epitome of wifely fidelity, tapestried for years while he was off to the wars and other manly pursuits. I guess she thought she would prove to him positively that she could not have been up to unwifely mischief while he was away. The results of her diligence and constancy were apparently there when he returned to delight his eye and reinforce his faith—yards and yards and yards of tapestry. Maybe if more men and women did needlepoint there wouldn't be war or even a population explosion!

So instead of calling it penelope, why don't they just call it duo canvas or double canvas? It is simply two horizontal, close-together threads woven over two vertical, close-together threads.

There are two types of canvas. This is knotted stitch done on mono 10.

This is the same stitch done on penelope 10.

Questions and Answers

1. What is the best canvas to use?

2. Which canvas do you prefer?

3. What color canvas is best to work on?

1. The "best" canvas to use is the one that will be the most serviceable for the design or plan to be worked.

2. I have no preference anymore. I use all types of canvas, simply because the piece I have designed dictates my choice.

3. Canvases usually come in white or shades of gray or beige. The very fine, that is the smallest-gauge, canvases to be found are in ecru or a very pale peach color. If your background color is white or a very pale pastel color, you should use only white canvas. But if your background or predominant colors are dark, it is best to use beige or gray canvas. It is very difficult to prevent the darker canvas threads from peeking out under white or light-colored yarn, particularly in any of the straight stitches. Similar problems arise when using white canvas under dark-colored yarns. Of course, if your design has a great range of colors—let's say from black and dark greens through soft yellows and pale blues, then you will have to make some kind of a compromise. But I am sure your best compromise will be beige canvas.

4. How do you decide what gauge canvas to use?

4. Now this answer will have to cover a lot of ground. Mono and penelope canvases come in a great variety of gauges. Gauge means the number of meshes, or threads, to an inch, which is how many stitches to the inch you will be working. Mono canvas is available from 10 (the largest holes) to 32 gauge. Personally, I prefer a smaller gauge than mono 10 (and that means a higher number). I find that a 10-gauge mono canvas can get very sleazy. Some people have better luck than I do.

Unless I am going to do very fine petit point (anything less than 16-gauge), my preference is 12, 14, or 16-gauge mono. These work more quickly for me, and I can accomplish fairly subtle shading. Penelope, of course, has more flexibility, and the range is far greater. An 8- or 10-gauge penelope canvas is stronger than the same gauge in mono because the double threads reinforce it. I have in my workroom a range of penelope canvases from 3½ to 16.

By flexibility, I mean the threads of a penelope canvas can be separated or split (see page 21), so 16 gauge can become 32, 12 becomes 24, and 10 becomes 20. A 3½ penelope canvas is woven almost like mono. The double threads are very tight and, therefore, difficult to separate. It is very good for what is called quick point. I prefer 5-point penelope canvas. The work goes quickly, and if I want to change the texture or tuck in a few smaller details, I can do so easily.

The decision as to which gauge canvas to use is dictated by the design, just how much delicacy of shading is desired, and how large the work will eventually be. For instance, at my time in life I would not attempt a piece 30 by 30 inches on 20-point mono canvas. Time is getting too precious! For the beginner, I suggest a fairly small project using 10-point penelope or 12-point mono canvas. This will not take too much time, and it will give you the real feel of the stitchery.

5. Of course! I do it all the time. More and more needle-pointers are using different stitchery on their canvases. It makes the work much more interesting, and the different effects and textures that result are fascinating, especially if you re-embroider over the stitches underneath. It should now be called needlepoint embroidery, since we have been released from the inflexibility of doing the serviceable but plain tent stitch or the half-cross stitch.

5. Can surface embroidery be attached to canvaswork?

6. As a rule, I have no rules. I work in a rather unorthodox fashion, but it works for me, and I find it easy.

When planning a bargello-type design, which is basically a form of non-planning, let's face it, I usually choose the colors and shades I want to use for the piece first. I have tried meticulously so many times to mark it all on graph paper, but I find myself getting tense and frustrated. I *know* it's never going to look that way on canvas. Then, too, I am going to have to go through the same routine all over again to count it out on the canvas anyway.

6. What is the easiest and best way to mark a canvas and what do you use?

What I usually do is mark the centers of the canvas horizontally and vertically, which will eventually also be an aid in blocking, and then count out from each center line in five and ten meshes or six and 12, depending on the shapes I eventually want—diamonds, rounded shapes, or up-and-down peaks.

I start at the center, working my needle in and out, up and down. That first row will determine the shapes that other rows will follow. You can then work with very little check on your counting, from the center down and then up, or out if you want mitered corners.

You will get surprises sometimes as you work. Then again, sometimes the shapes work better than you had imagined, if you have counted and marked very precisely.

Marking canvases that range from 10 to 5 point can easily be done with a waterproof marker. But when you get to the finer-mesh gauges I have found it safer and clearer to use a contrasting color of sewing thread, doubled, going in and out of the canvas with a small basting stitch. And you can stitch right over the basting stitches with your yarn. The sewing thread will never show through.

If you are working with light-colored yarns and use a marker, the markings can bleed or show through your stitchery. And you will never be able to eliminate that disturbing look. I rarely use the most commonly-known felt marker because it makes too heavy a line, which tends to show through the needlepoint.

If I can find it, I often use a fine-point felt marker that is *indelible*. These markers come in a wide range of very soft shades, which are more than adequate to guide you through your work. Never use a black marker.

Best of all, and the cheapest (I do get stingy about some things), is the ballpoint laundry marker. These can be found in stationery and hardware stores or at the sewing counter in department stores. They make a fine light line and are waterproof and indelible. Just be careful not to lean too heavily when you are marking with it. If you have a delicate canvas, the ballpoint might cut a thread.

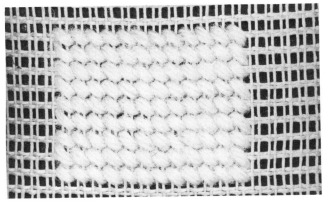

Half-cross stitch. See directions on page 117. This stitch cannot be done on mono canvas.

Gauge is the number of meshes per inch. This is oblique stitch (discussed in Chapter 3) done on 10-point penelope.

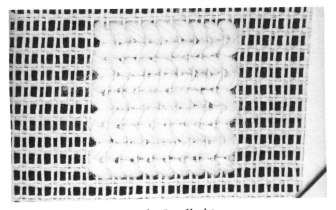

Reverse half-cross stitch. I call this the lazy knit stitch. It is made by reversing the direction of the half-cross stitch every row, and must also be done on penelope.

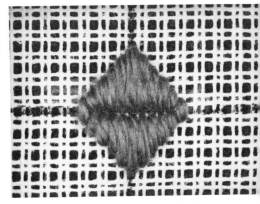

This is triangle stitch (described in Chapter 4) done on 5-point penelope. You can see that the penelope 5 has meshes twice as big as the penelope 10.

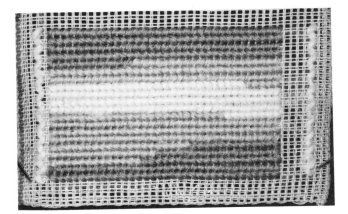

If you make a guide at the edge of the canvas, you will never make a mistake about the direction of the lazy knit stitch.

39

Project 1 (page 26)

I had a commission for a 24 by 24-inch ottoman. I knew the room and the house it was going into very well. It had to be very fine, and again there was a birthday deadline to meet. I had a postcard from the Albert and Victoria Museum in London that had drawings of very imaginative and strange-looking wildflowers on it. I did several sketches of these and then did my cut-out trick.

I placed cut-outs of the wildflowers around the graph paper until I found the placement that pleased me. Well, I knew the flowers *had* to be done in petit point, but at the same time, I also wanted a strong and not too delicate effect. So I chose a 12-point penelope canvas. Naturally, I split the threads for the flowers, which were done in tent stitch (see page 21), with French knots to emphasize the centers.

I continued the petit point stitchery all around the flowers for five or six rows so that the larger stitches of the background would not crowd into the flowers. The flowers were done in silk and the background in Persian wool yarn using the diagonal tent stitch, also known as the basketweave stitch.

I had already marked my canvas for the border. That's where I started making time. For the border I used what is really an improvisation of the straight Gobelin stitch.

The straight Gobelin stitch looks very much like bargello. But I suppose whenever you have straight stitches that go up and down in points, it more or less becomes bargello.

Designing by arranging cut-out sketches on a piece of marked graph paper. The sketches were adapted from pictures on a postcard.

40

Stitches of surface embroidery can be done over needlepoint stitches for a decorative effect. The French knot is begun by bringing the needle to the front of the work, at the chosen place, through previous stitchery. Lay the needle almost flat against the work, and wrap yarn around needle completely, in the direction away from you.

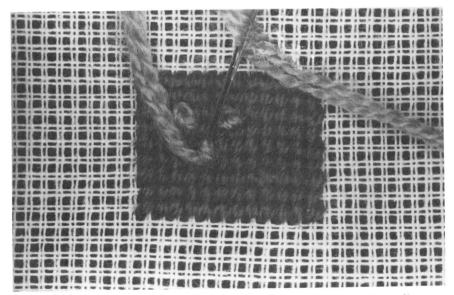

French knot, *step 2*. Push needle through small loop that is around it, and right through to back of work, in one motion, thus making a small knot on the surface.

Various French knots, made by winding once, twice, or three times around the needle.

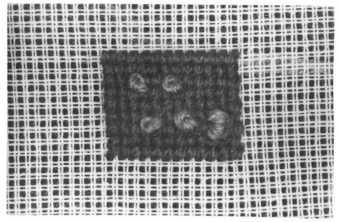

Diagonal tent stitch. See directions on page 118.

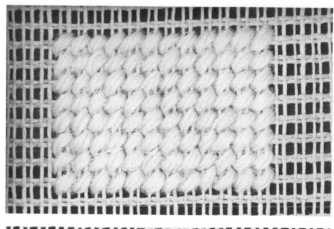

Back view of diagonal tent stitch. The basket weave, resulting from the diagonal method of working the stitch, gives added padding.

Another canvas marked for bargello. The border is really an improvisation on straight Gobelin stitch (see Chapter 4), and was used on the wildflower ottoman.

42

Project 2 (page 26)

Some years ago, while playing *Barefoot in the Park* outside of Baltimore, I was prowling around in an antique shop and found a very interesting little footstool. It had bamboo legs that fascinated me, but it was very badly upholstered. Since I had just bought a home in the country, I thought it would be good to have on hand for some future needlepoint.

It stumbled around my house from room to room. I just couldn't make a decision about what to do with the footstool. Fortunately, my good and dear friends, the Merrells (Jan Miner) came for brunch.

Dick has always been sneaky about spying in my workroom. I had been fumbling about trying to plan a very traditional bargello design, sometimes called tulip, sometimes pineapple. The way I eventually handled it, I prefer to call it pineapple. Dick was wild about it.

His enthusiasm gave me both an idea and the impetus to do it. Their tenth anniversary was approaching. (Yes, the marriage I wrote about in the chapter, "Waste Not, Want Not—A Love Story," in my first book has lasted and is going stronger than ever!) The antique footstool would suit their home to a T.

It was simple to make the adjustment from the square of my original plan to the oblong top of the footstool. The three of us are compulsive about our preference for muted autumnal colors with touches of bright orange. So the choice of colors didn't take much effort. Since the footstool was small, 12 by 18 inches, I naturally chose a finer gauge canvas. I used 16-point mono. I selected the colors in three-ply Persian yarn, using only two strands of it. To set off the pineapple effect, I did diagonal tent stitch (see page 42) between the motifs instead of continuing the bargello stitch.

A bargello design sometimes called tulip, sometimes pineapple. The stool was done on 16-point mono, the pillow adaptation of the same design on 5-point penelope with rug wool.

43

Project 3 (page 27)

For my own amusement, I wondered what the design of the footstool covering would look like if I went to the other extreme and did it on 5-point penelope canvas using rug wool. Well, I think the result is successful, and it suits my house just fine. It is interesting that the change of canvas and wool can make the same design take on an entirely different effect.

Actually, the counting and working of bargello on 5-point penelope is different than it would be on any smaller-gauge penelope canvas. In order to cover successfully a 5-point canvas with a straight up-and-down bargello stitch, as opposed to a slanting stitch like tent, you must treat the canvas as if it were 10-point mono. In other words, you must go a half mesh down in the same manner as separating threads of a canvas.

Sometimes, when you are working on a large piece in 5-point canvas especially, you wish you had three hands. It is very difficult when you are working the center of the piece. It can be very awkward to hold and work at the same time. But if you remember to work from the center out to the edges, it will go quickly, and the piece won't feel so heavy. Before you know it, it's finished.

Bargello on 5-point penelope must be worked by splitting the double threads, or it will not cover successfully.

Marking a fine-gauge (16 point or finer) canvas with basting thread instead of a marker. I usually use a basting stitch in a compatible shade of thread. The basting can be ripped out as the stitching progresses, or it can be left to be covered by the stitching.

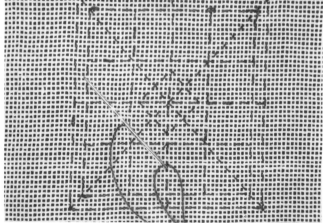

44

3
What Is the Best Yarn to Use?

Now we come to a very large dilemma. When it comes to yarn, there are so many choices. And you will hear the word "ply" used a great deal: two-ply, three-ply, four-ply. You will soon learn that the term "ply" can sometimes be very misleading.

Rug yarn, which is very thick, is four-ply. Yet there is a very fine tapestry yarn that is also four-ply. Unless you double or triple it, it can only be used well on 18 or 20-point canvas.

Persian yarn is generally three-ply. When it is separated, a single strand can be used for petit point. Even that is sometimes too thick for the finer canvases. So you can see ply really has nothing to do with the thickness of the yarn, as most people think. Ply has to do with the number of strands twisted into the yarn. There is a very fine crewel wool that has a lovely texture and works beautifully for fine petit point or re-embroidering over needlepoint stitches.

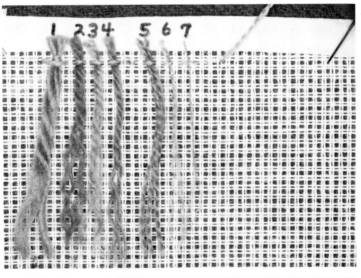

This shows how deceiving the word "ply" can be. No. 1 is rug wool. Nos. 2, 3, and 4 are what is usually called needlepoint or tapestry yarn. These first four are all four-ply, but vary greatly in thickness. No. 5 is Persian which is three-ply. Nos. 6 and 7 are very fine crewel yarn; both are two-ply, yet No. 7 is only half as thick as No. 6.

Here are five different silks. As with wools, there is a great variance in weight and ply, and the choice must be made according to the canvas, the design, and the effect you are trying to achieve.

Underwater hot hippo; see chapter 3, project 2

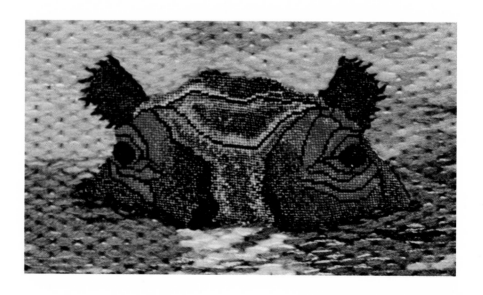

Wastebaskets and tissue boxes, with wallpapers that inspired designs; see chapter 3, project 3 and chapter 6

Questions and Answers

1. Do you use what is called needlepoint yarn?

1. I always use needlepoint, or tapestry, yarn. I never use knitting wools. They are much too springy for needlepoint, plus the fact that knitting yarns will not take the abrasion of the stitchery against the canvas. The fibers break down.

2. Do you ever combine different types of yarn?

2. Ah, yes! many, many times have I combined different types of yarn. This is when choices begin to make sense to me. And this is when the fun begins and you let your creativity fly. Of course, combining yarns depends completely on the canvas and the design. Sometimes what I am doing does not call for the combining of yarns.

3. Is the weight or thickness of yarn the same throughout your pieces?

3. Well, that depends. I have used several different thicknesses of yarn and different types of yarn in one piece of needlepoint. But the choice depends on the color and shade availability and the effect I wish to create—and achieve.

4. Please tell us how you envision color contrasts in the yarns you choose?

4. What I envision in color contrasts is dictated by the painting or drawing of the design. I have learned, though, not to expect too much when translating a painting, drawing, or photograph into needlepoint. It is almost impossible to get the fineness of shading you hoped for or to achieve the foreshortening that you can get in a painting or drawing. The contrasts must be quite sharp so you can get separation—between leaves, or petals, or a leg or a paw of an animal. Whenever I am stumped for the right result, and I realize that I have set an impossible goal for myself, I use grass, leaves, flowers or something like that in the foreground to block out the impossible problem area.

5. Unfortunately, I have never been able in all these years to figure out how much of a color of yarn I will need for a design. That's the formula that has somehow escaped me! To tell the truth, I have a mathematical mental block that makes it useless for me to try. Usually I trust my eye, but that's no guaranteed estimate. So, like a lot of people, I usually over-buy, mainly because too often I have had the frustration of a discontinued dye lot. Even if the dye lot is the same number, I have had the double frustration that the shade of color is slightly different. This is almost hair-tearing time. And that is the reason why I have often changed or altered a background to do what I call a toned-down or *ombréd* (shaded) background, which I will discuss in two projects in this chapter. If I do run out of a shade, I can always tone-in another shade. It is a marvelous effect for water or sky, and it eliminates the static look some pieces have.

Here's another little trick I've learned. If a background shade is a little off, instead of working back and forth across the canvas, reverse the slant of the stitch at the center and at the corners. Each pie-shaped section will have its own tone when light hits it. This is best illustrated in the ottoman with wildflowers and the bargello border, shown on page 26.

5. How do you determine how much yarn of a single color you will need for a design?

Opposite
Oriental pillows on different gauge
canvases; see chapter 4, project 2 (below),
and chapter 4, project 3 (above)

My "Feelies" pillow; see chapter 4, project 1

50

Project 1 (page 2)

One day on the set while filming *Do Not Spindle, Fold or Mutilate*, Helen Hayes, Myrna Loy, Mildred Natwick, and I were sitting in a row waiting for the next camera set-up. Helen was thumbing through my first book. Myrna had her script in her lap. Millie was staring at me as if I were some creature from Mars. I was working on my peripatetic zebra, and had completed the head and almost all of the body.

I looked at them and at myself, too. What were we really thinking? We are four women, who some 30-odd years before had performed in some very important film classics that had been filmed at this very same studio: Helen and Myrna in Samuel Goldwyn's *Arrowsmith*, Myrna in *The Best Years of Our Lives*, Millie in John Ford's *Long Voyage Home*, and me in *Street Scene, Dead End, You Only Live Once*, with Henry Fonda (who does fine needlepoint, but I wish he weren't so reluctant to exhibit his paintings—he is brilliant!), and *Blood on the Sun* with James Cagney.

What was going through their minds? The building that once housed our plush dressing rooms was now all for business offices. Instead of the hairdressers and makeup crew coming to us, we arrived at 5:30 or 6 a.m. to be "done" in a communal makeup and hairdressing department. Our dressing rooms were now temporary trailers that moved from stage to stage depending upon where the set we were filming was located. The studio that once teemed and bustled with activity now had many ghost sound stages.

Somehow none of us ever discussed any of this. But I looked at their eyes, and I knew what they were thinking. Helen was checking up on me in my book. Myrna was looking out of the corners of *those* eyes wondering, "How have you got the patience to do all that?" And Millie's stare was explained. Yes, eyes are important and tell a lot.

Invariably, with the animal studies that I have done, I am questioned about the expression of the eyes. I learned a lesson about that from the Duchess of Windsor some years ago. She bought a piece I had done which I called *The Cross-Eyed Owl*. It was a white owl, with wings fully spread, discovering a four-leaf clover. After a few days, she returned it. She said it made her nervous, because the bird seemed about to pounce on the tiny plant.

Ever since then, I have tried to do any animal or bird that I design and execute in characteristically relaxed positions, either well-fed or sleepy. They are much easier to live with.

52

Or else, I do baby animals discovering something for the first time. Did you ever watch a puppy discovering a butterfly or a dandelion for the first time? Or a puppy seeing snow for the first time? That's the expression I try to reproduce. That's why I always do the head and the eyes first. It gives me a clue as to how the rest of the piece will work. I have also done a lot of staring at the portraits of famous painters, concentrating on the eyes. From this I have learned to put a small pearl or a crystal bead in the eyes of the animals I do. It helps to catch the light and increase the brightness of the eye.

The peripatetic baby zebra is approximately 22 by 24 inches and is done on a 10-point penelope canvas. For the baby I used mostly very fine four-ply tapestry wool split in half to fit the split threads of the canvas. The butterfly is on a small piece of 30-point mono, worked in a single thread of silk, and woven into the larger canvas. (More about this technique later in Chapter 5.) The marshy ground and rocks are done in the diagonal mosaic stitch.

The entire sky is done in the oblique stitch, which is like a slanting Gobelin stitch (see page 28) gone crazy.

Acetates, rayons, and acrylics are less expensive and more easily available than silk, but I am always fearful of the results because of one bad experience. If silk is unavailable, I would rather substitute a good cotton embroidery floss. It has a nice sheen and works beautifully for petit-point detail. It gives a slight kick to other stitchery. Any metallic threads you use should be checked for heat, and the piece should be blocked carefully.

I re-embroidered over some of the petit point stitchery in the hind leg and baby's rear end. Those two parts nearly had me crazy! I couldn't get the depth I wanted because the hoof of the hind leg is in the extreme foreground of the piece and the crook of the hind leg and the rear end go further into the background. The re-embroidery did the trick and gave me the depth perception I wanted. For the sky I mixed some very fine tapestry wool, crewel yarn, and a single strand of Persian in one needle in various shades. I didn't want the tree to look bare, and I still didn't want every leaf accounted for, so I mixed various shades of green and blended them into the background. There was never any danger of running out of any shade or color, because I could always blend something into it and keep the continuity.

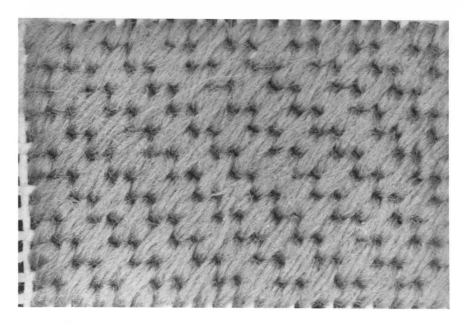

Diagonal mosaic stitch. See directions
on page 121.

Oblique stitch. See directions on
page 122.

Project 2 (page 46)

The original sketch of the underwater hippopotamus was printed in my first book. At that time I was so involved with the writing of the book and the photography, there was absolutely no time to execute the hippo in needlepoint before publication. So the sketch was tucked neatly away in my "file and forget" portfolio.

One morning there was a telephone call from a gentleman who shall remain nameless. "Miss Sidney," he said, "the hippo on page 22 in your book, is it available?"

"I've never done it," I replied.

"But it's in your book!" he exclaimed. How could I possibly explain all the steps between sketch and finished needlepoint to him on the phone? He said he wanted it to give it as a wedding present. Another deadline, I thought to myself. The price he said he would pay for it bolted me right across the room to my "file and forget" portfolio. I found the sketch in a hurry.

The underwater hippo is approximately 12 by 18 inches in size. The head is in silk on 24-point mono canvas. This gauge gave me more flexibility in working the head and ears with two strands of silk in two different tones in the needle. This piece of canvas was woven into the background canvas, which is 12-point mono (see Chapter 5 for more about petit-point insertion).

The head is executed in tent stitch and the water and sky are done in oblique stitch (see page 54). I mixed pale greens, very pale blues, and a little pink for the sky, using some tapestry yarn, some crewel, and Persian in one needle. To emphasize the waterline, I naturally had to go to darker and stronger colors. But for the highlight on the water, I mixed some pale blue and white silk in the same needle. The border is done in a knotted stitch.

Even in the border I mixed the shades. I wanted the impression that the sky and water went on *ad infinitum*. The real finishing touch to this piece, however, is two black jet beads, one in each eye of the hippo. They give highlights to the eyes and a teary look from the bright, hot sun.

Project 3 (page 47)

Kathryne Hays is a neighbor and good friend of mine. She is an editor of *Vogue* magazine. Several years ago she bought an old four-story house up here in Connecticut. The house was originally an old mill.

Kay has put a lot of time, thought, love, and money into the place. But she has also put something else into it—taste, the thing this gal has plenty of.

Some time back she had a birthday coming up, and I wanted to do something in needlepoint for her lovely house. One of her bathrooms is done in pinks, oranges, and black, based on a Marimekko design. I designed a facial-tissue box cover to go in that bathroom.

I used two shades of orange and white Persian wool yarn. I didn't have a good strong black, but I found some black crochet cotton and used it doubled on the 10-point penelope canvas. It is done in the half-cross stitch (see page 39) and the Old Florentine stitch.

I whizzed through this little piece while waiting in my dressing room in Chicago, where I was playing in Tennessee Williams' *Suddenly Last Summer* with Katherine Houghton, the niece and namesake of Katherine Hepburn, and a true reflection of her marvelous aunt.

One night, Katherine Hepburn flew into Chicago and came to the theatre unannounced. We didn't even know she was in the audience. In fact, we were on our way back to our dressing rooms after our curtain calls when we heard the audience break out into loud applause. We wondered what that was all about. We just shrugged and went on our way. They were applauding Kate, the aunt.

The talented niece brought her famous aunt into my dressing room. She was most flattering about my performance as Mrs. Venable, the part she had played in the screen version of the play, and she was thrilled to hear me say how much I admired and enjoyed playing with her niece.

Before I finish this chapter, I would like to make one suggestion. When you have begun a needlepoint project, don't let too much time elapse between working periods. You will not only lose your impetus, you will lose the idea you originally had in mind. That happened to me with the baby zebra, and it became more and more difficult for me to finally finish it. More about that later.

56

Old Florentine stitch. See directions on page 123.

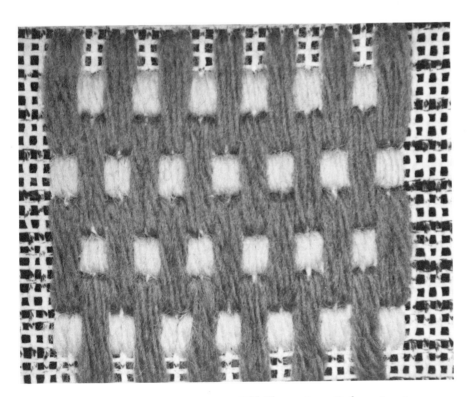

Old Florentine stitch, using two colors. See directions for this variation on page 125.

4
Can Needlepoint Cause Eyestrain?

Strangely enough, this chapter seems to have the fewest questions, but possibly—and subliminally—it will answer more questions than you can conceive. It deals, of course, with needlepoint. But it also deals with what was perhaps the most trying and frightening time in my life.

Questions and Answers

1. I think, without any doubt, needlepoint is most certainly therapy. For me, and for millions of women and men, it is a most relaxing activity, and a most rewarding one. Once you get the hang of the stitchery and become more proficient, the rhythm of needlepoint is soothing. You can listen to music and enjoy conversation while you are doing it. And when you get really good and are working with a stitch that is easy for you, you can even peek at television. I have watched some young girls stitch away at a fast pace while barely looking at their canvases. But this takes some practicing.

2. I have some good days and some bad days, like all arthritics. I have found that if I do some needlepoint, pretty soon I forget the pain, instead of continuing to moan about it.

3. If you play too many sets of tennis, quite naturally you feel strain in your arms and legs. This is true of anything you overdo. I guess it depends on the individual, but personally I have never felt any eyestrain from needlepoint. And I've been known to work eight to ten hours at a stretch, with only short coffee breaks. Yes, of course, my leg or foot has gone to sleep or my back-aches. But that's my own fault. More importantly, when you settle down to do needlepoint, make sure you have a comfortable chair, perhaps even a footstool, and good light. Use your hands for the needlepoint but use your head to plan your working time—pace yourself to allow for rest periods.

4. Absolutely not! My two eye operations had nothing to do with my needlepoint whatsoever. The surgery on my eyes was for a very common flaw in nature—cataracts. Although this condition is usually associated with the elderly, even babies have been known to be born with cataracts. I was told a long time ago that cataracts were developing in each of my eyes. But no doctor can foretell how rapidly they will develop or how soon surgery might be necessary.

1. Is needlepoint therapy?

2. I understand you have arthritis. If this is true, how does it affect your needlepoint?

3. Have you ever had any eyestrain problems due to needlepoint?

4. Recently I read that you had some kind of eye surgery. Was this caused by your needlepoint work?

Years went by, and I wasn't disturbed or bothered by the condition. I passed driver's tests with no difficulty. My designing and needlepointing continued without discomfort. But during the filming of *Do Not Spindle, Fold or Mutilate*, I noticed that it became increasingly difficult for me to remain in bright sunlight, and driving at night was out of the question. The poor baby zebra was rolled up and put aside. I began working on larger-mesh canvases and using larger stitchery. That's the main reason why all the commercial kits I designed were on 10-point and 5-point canvas.

By the time I returned home to Connecticut, I realized that I was seeing everything through gray chiffon. After consulting my eye doctor, I got the bad news—right between my nonseeing eyes. No prescription for glasses would help. Surgery was the only answer. And I had to give up smoking. The doctor would not operate unless I did. This was a time of many adjustments for me.

I had smoked incessantly since I was 15 years old. Which was more important, the possibility of my sight being restored, or giving up a habit that I was already beginning to think was rather nasty? Well, I tossed away the two packages of cigarettes in my purse. The commitment was made. I wanted that surgery desparately, almost as much as life itself. Giving up smoking made me worse than a witch on a broomstick for quite awhile. I will always be eternally grateful for the patience of my dear and close friends. That they continued to speak to me during this period is more than a miracle.

At long last, I was scheduled for surgery on my left eye. The fear, the panic the night before is indescribable. But after the bandage was removed, and I had my first eyeglasses, I could see color again, could see the faces of those good friends again. It was a marvelous and beautiful thing. (And I really never knew how good looking my doctor was until that time.) My impatience to have the right eye operated on as quickly as possible must have been quite a trying thing for my doctor.

Between the two operations though, I managed to design five commercial kits and plan the stitchery for the kits and film a a television commercial. The night before the filming the director telephoned and told me he would like it very much if I could be doing some needlepoint while delivering the commercial message.

As soon as I hung up I went up to my workroom, hauled out some 5-point canvas, marked the center by drawing horizontal, vertical and diagonal lines (see page 82). I picked out some rug wools, using the colors the director suggested. I sat down and began to do some stitching. I had decided on the herringbone stitch (see page 64), because it works quickly.

I sat bolt upright. I suddenly realized that my right eye was practically sightless, and without those thick-lensed glasses I would not see with my recently operated-on left eye! What was I to do? I couldn't be photographed with those heavy lenses. It was getting late. I had to be up at six in the morning because the crew was arriving at 7:30. Well, I propped myself up in bed, with canvas and wools, and started to practice by feeling.

As I was packing the next morning to return to the hospital for my second operation, I impulsively grabbed the almost bare canvas and a bagful of wool. I cannot imagine what made me feel so optimistic. The second operation was a breeze. I knew what to expect, and most of all, I had no fear. The recuperation period is what is so taxing and boring. The inactivity drove me right up the wall.

One morning, walking restlessly about my hospital room, I remembered the canvas and the wool. I thought, what's to lose? I could see with my left eye. My right eye was still bandaged. If I could work by feeling for the commercial, why not with the sight of one eye wearing those thick glasses? Some time later, one of the nurses came into my room to check on something. She almost fainted. "What do you think you're doing?" she cried, as she looked at the mess of wool on the floor and the canvas on my lap.

"Oh," I said, "Nobody told me not to do it, and I bet I'll finish it before I leave the hospital!" This story traveled through the hospital with such speed that before I knew it, I could have held needlepoint seminars every day in my room. I called this particular piece my *Feelies Pillow*. It's perfect except for one mistake I made in counting. I don't know how it happened, except that possibly my needle is quicker than my eye. I was not about to do all the ripping it would take to make the correction. Mistake and all, the canvas *was* finished when I was ready to leave the hospital.

Project 1 (page 50)

I am rather sentimental about my *Feelies Pillow*. It measures 24 by 24 inches and is on 5-point penelope canvas. As I said before, it was completely improvised from start to finish. With my handicap, I couldn't make too rigid a plan or design, and I wasn't too careful when I stuffed all those wools into that bag. It is really an exercise in improvisation. I used the herringbone stitch from one step to four step.

Some of the stitches are over two meshes and some of them over four meshes, with rug wool or three-ply Persian, doubled. The colors are four shades of green, two of rust and jonquil yellow and beige. I used the half-cross stitch (see page 39) in some of the corners to even up the stitchery. I suppose at the time I was really only interested in color, the blending and toning of shade, because seeing color was such a spectacular experience for me.

The one area where I miscounted—I still cannot figure out how—I thought I could blend with some of the muted shades. Then I thought, that's a cop-out. A mistake is a mistake, admit it, show it, emphasize it! So, I used coral-ish henna to bring it out. As I look at the piece now, I smile a great deal, because I even had the nerve to sign and date it, before I left the hospital.

After several months, I was able to wear contact lenses, and what a bright world it is! In the last two years I have played all over the country in stock, in dinner theatres, in regional theatres. I was really on the go doing *Butterflies Are Free*, *Barefoot in the Park* again and again, *Suddenly Last Summer*, *Arsenic and Old Lace*, the movie *Summer Wishes, Winter Dreams* starring Joanne Woodward and Martin Balsam, and a new play for the Seattle Repertory Theatre.

While I was in Seattle, I met a charming and giving man, an antiquarian and collector of fine old Oriental rugs. After seeing some of his collection of rugs, I got an idea. How about using needlepoint to adapt an old Oriental rug design, and using very simple stitchery for very diverse projects?

Herringbone stitch variations. See directions for two-step herringbone on page 102. This is two-step herringbone over 3 meshes.

Two-step herringbone over 5 meshes.

These three pictures show sequential stages of three different herringbone variations. The top row of each is two-step herringbone over 4 meshes. The center row is three-step herringbone over 4 meshes. The bottom row is four-step herringbone over 3 meshes. For each "step" you can add another color, achieving a great variety of effects. But using just one shade gives a heavy, braided texture that I sometimes like for framing the edge of a piece.

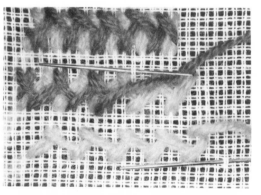

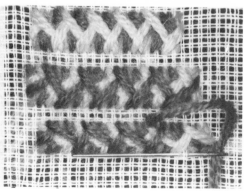

Project 2 (page 51)

My plan was to make a pillow cover using the traditional Chinese coin motif, but give the border the most emphasis. I used 16-point mono canvas and two-ply Persian yarn. The reason that I deviated from the traditional coloring found in Chinese rugs was because beiges, rusts, and soft greens best suit my living room. I wanted the piece to be 16 by 16 inches simply because I already had a ready-made velvet pillow that size.

As I have explained before, 16-gauge mono is too fine to mark with a marker, so I used the small basting-stitch method to indicate the horizontal, vertical and diagonal lines (page 44). I then counted carefully from the center out and stitched the outer-edge boundaries.

Since I wanted to emphasize the importance of the border, I worked from the edges in, toward the center. I am really very much opposed to this procedure, as I have said, because an error in counting can be a disaster. Believe me, I found out!

After I had finished the border and studied it, it occurred to me that an endless variety of little things could be made, varying the colors, but using the pattern of the stitchery. Belts, luggage-rack straps, hatbands, brick doorstop covers—just about anything you could name. I did not want the coin motif to look too specific. I just wanted the idea of it, so I used a form of Scotch stitch. It is really just four halves of a Scotch stitch.

Doing the background was a bit of a problem. Because of working from the outer edges toward the center, the mitered corners did not quite match. They did not have a neat, clear look. Well, that little illness can be easily cured. It can be done by compromising—just as you would use small stitches to blend petit point with gros point. Sometimes these are called compensation stitches. I prefer to call them ad-lib stitches. Just as in the theatre, actors will ad lib to cover an error—the phone or doorbell that fails to ring, the pistol that doesn't shoot or the actor (heaven help him!) who fails to appear.

So the ad-lib stitch, or a couple of them tucked in wherever necessary, can cover an unsatisfactory area without distressing the innocent viewer whatsoever. So I "covered" the messy miters with small back stitches, matching each color as they met at each corner. In addition to the Scotch stitch, the only other stitch I used is an improvisation of the Old Florentine stitch (see page 57).

Scotch stitch variation I used in the oriental-coin pillow. See directions on page 105. In my previous book I called this variation "5".

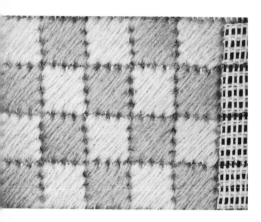

Scotch stitch variation "1" uses two colors in a checkerboard effect.

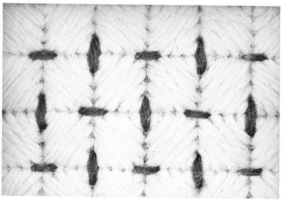

Scotch stitch variation "2" is Scotch stitch reversed. The stitch is done diagonally in opposite directions, with stitches added at the corners of the squares. The possible combinations of color are infinite.

Scotch stitch variation "3". To do this, work the stitch diagonally in opposite directions. Skip a step in each square; then fill it in with a contrasting color or shade.

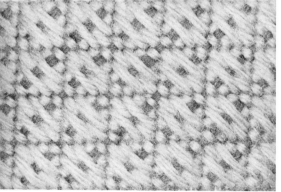

Scotch stitch variation "6". Work the stitch diagonally (see page 106). Then take yarn in a sharply contrasting color and weave it in and out through the squares.

Project 3 (page 51)

I liked the result of the Chinese coin motif very much. I also liked the simplicity of the design and the stitchery. So I though, why not a rug?

Naturally, to repeat the design precisely was practically impossible on 5-point penelope canvas, due primarily to the variance of the canvases. The counting had to be adjusted, and the Scotch stitch seemed too clumsy. I do a lot of experimenting with stitches before I begin to work on the actual piece. I call these my rehearsal stitches.

The Scotch stitch looked terrible. I wanted to get the same effect. And after rehearsing several different stitches, I finally decided to use a double triangle, which when broken down is really just straight Gobelin increased from 1 mesh to 5 meshes and then decreased to 1 mesh again.

The spacing is relatively the same. Also I used more subtle toning in the same colors, because when working so large an area, I didn't want the results to look too "busy." I worked this one, too, from the edges to the center. And I promised myself that if I could possibly avoid it, I will never work this way again!

I left the edges unfinished, in case I wanted to continue with more 24 by 24-inch squares. I call this idea "make-a-pillow, start-a-rug." You can make several of these big pillows in no time at all. Leave the border unfinished, fold back at least 1½ inches of canvas and blind-stitch it to a ready-made pillow the same size.

Then if you wish to continue with the start-a-rug idea, you can join the squares together as you complete them. This is explained in question 6 of the next chapter. You can have a rug—small, large, any size you want—or you can end up with a runner, depending on your desire or what use you want to put it to. If making all those squares begins to bore you, well, stop where you are and pile all those big pillows on a sofa or on the floor. I think it's an absolutely smashing look!

Triangle stitch, a variation of the straight Gobelin. See directions for the Gobelin on page 105. When working triangle stitch on 5-point penelope, move up and down $\frac{1}{2}$ mesh, splitting the double threads, from right to left or left to right. Be sure to mark the centers horizontally and vertically. In this triangle, the height is 3 meshes, so move up $\frac{1}{2}$ mesh 6 times and down $\frac{1}{2}$ mesh 5 times to complete the top. For the bottom triangle, move down $\frac{1}{2}$ mesh 5 times and up $\frac{1}{2}$ mesh 4 times to meet your first stitch.

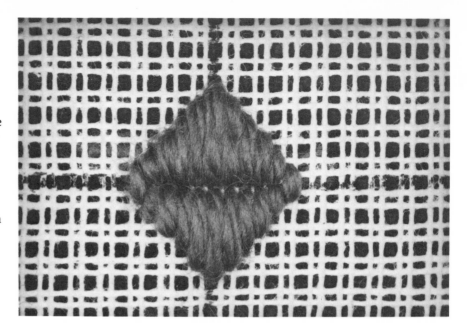

The basic, and simplest, of the straight up-and-down stitches is Gobelin. It covers large (or small) areas very quickly, and the texture of it is quite beautiful. Depending on the effect desired, it can be worked over 2, 3, 4, or 5 meshes. It is very easy to do if you mark the canvas as illustrated.

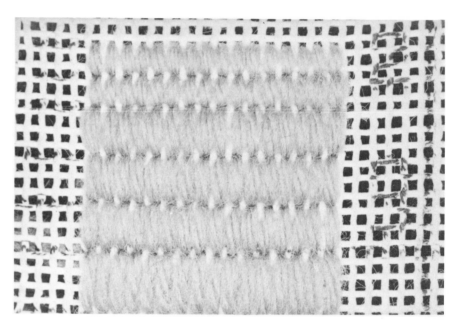

68

5
How Do You Block Needlepoint, and How Do You Join Canvases?

I have tried, so far, with all the questions to confine them and the answers to very specific areas. As I said before, some of the areas overlap, so if I seem repetitious, it is because the questions that I have been asked overlap and have pertinence to other areas of needlepoint. In this chapter, I have opened my Pandora's box of questions and let them all fall out helter-skelter. Hopefully the answers will be helpful and solve some of your needlepoint problems.

Lost monkey and friends; see chapter 5, project 1 and chapter 6

Lost monkey and original sketch, see chapter 1

Opposite
Petit-point sunflower with beaded center, inserted on larger gauge canvas; see chapter 5

70

Questions and Answers

1. Should a beginner master a variety of stitches before actually starting a specific piece?

1. Please, just tell me why should you master a lot of different stitches without a focal point? It would be like learning piano exercises without the goal of finally playing a tune. If you work on a piece, instead of abstract practicing stitches, you will see progress and improvement. And you will have that great satisfying feeling of accomplishment, of getting something done and seeing the results of your time and effort. With that wonderful feeling, you can go on to other stitchery, not necessarily more complicated.

The answer to this question, then, is that I'm all for jumping right in and starting on an actual piece. Don't forget, you can always do those rehearsal stitches at the edge of the canvas, which will eventually be out of sight when your stitching has been completed and the piece is finished.

2. How do you carry your work around? Doesn't it require a lot of room?

2. The amount of room required to carry your needlepoint along with you naturally depends on the size of the piece you are working on. The average piece can be carried in a large purse or a small tote bag. I don't like to fold the canvas. It makes an awful crease, and when you stitch in the folded area, you will find that the sizing has softened and the meshes have lost their squareness. If you save the cardboard tubing from paper towels, waxed paper, or aluminum foil, you can roll your canvas around one of them. It doesn't take more room. And your canvas won't have the bends!

3. Do you ever use a frame when working, and doesn't a frame keep the canvas in shape, thus eliminating the necessity of blocking?

3. I rarely use a frame, because it's too clumsy to carry around. I use a frame when the piece is very large. A large piece would be heavy and uncomfortable to work draped over my lap and the floor. Besides, using a frame is no guarantee that the piece won't have to be blocked. The tension you work with really determines how out of shape the piece will be and how much blocking will be needed. Try to work in an even, relaxed manner, so that the stitches have a slight puffiness. If you yank and tug on every stitch, the canvas will peek through your stitches, and the work will be terribly misshapen.

While on the subject of tension, I would like to make a suggestion about the length of yarn or thread you work with. Although many instructions suggest a piece of yarn about 18 inches long, I strongly advise much less—a piece about 12 or 14 inches long. When you work with very long yarn, your elbows, neck, and shoulders will feel as though you've had a masterful karate chop! When you work with shorter yarn, your speed increases, you are not so apt to pull your stitches too tightly, and the last few inches of your yarn won't fray so much.

One more small suggestion while we are discussing little techniques to make work easier. Wool and silk have a tendency to curl as you work, and curled thread produces flat stitches that don't cover the canvas fully. One way of ensuring that this doesn't happen is to let the needle drop and hang free. It will uncurl. As you become more proficient, you will begin, almost unconsciously, to twirl the needle a quarter or a half turn every few stitches.

4. The preparation of a canvas, before the design is transferred onto it, is a thing that I am very old-fashioned about. After you have decided what the outside measurements of your finished piece will be, cut the canvas at least an inch-and-a-half or, better still, two inches larger on all four sides.

4. How do you prepare your canvas before working?

I don't particularly like the masking-tape method of edging a canvas to prevent unraveling. I consider it a waste of time. After working on the piece for several hours, the tape will peel away, your canvas will start to unravel after all, and you will only have to retape it. Besides, the tape will not hold up for doing a proper blocking job.

Instead of taping, I prefer to make a small hem on all four sides, either by hand or zig-zag machine stitching. It takes no more time than the taping method, and there is no danger of the canvas unraveling. Plus, you will have a good firm edge for tacks when you are ready to block the piece.

My friend Kidd's Ladybug, petit-point
insertion with bargello border and
fringe; see chapter 5

74

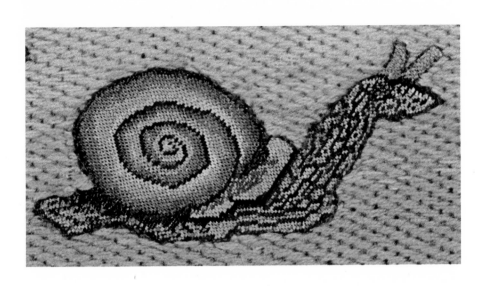

Snails, petit-point insertion with triangle-stitch border and oblique-stitch background; see chapter 5

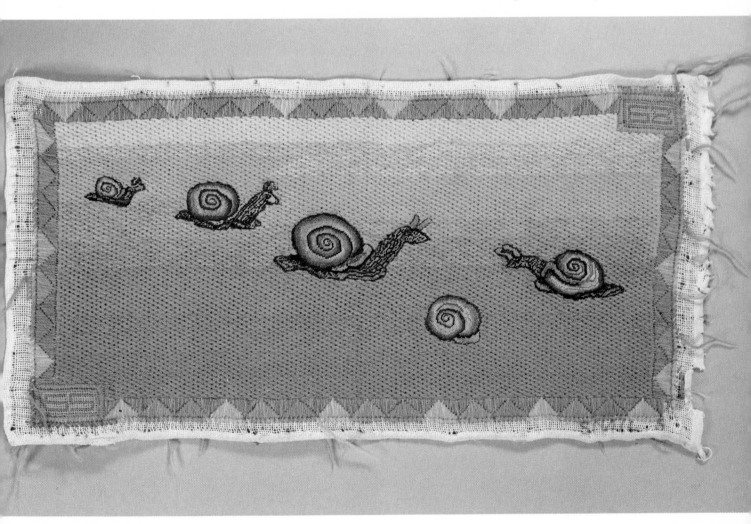

Then, no matter what the design is, I *always* do one thing. I fold my canvas in half, and mark the centers of all four edges lightly with a ball-point laundry marker. This finds the true center of the canvas. If the piece is quite large, I mark it in thirds or quarters, horizontally and vertically. If the piece is very misshapen when finished, these lines then become invaluable guides for blocking. You'd be surprised how your eye can deceive you about the straightness of canvas. Believe me, these guide lines will undeceive you.

5. How do you block your needlepoint?

5. Blocking is another procedure that I am really very stuffy about. There are many methods suggested, but I rigidly stick to the method that follows, because it absolutely ensures a good blocking result.

First of all, I wash the piece in a good fine-fabric soap. Before I end up doing a commercial, may I suggest you treat it as you would a very fine wool sweater. Wash it in cool water, rinse it many times, then roll it in a Turkish towel to remove the excess water. *Don't wring it!*

You will be amazed at the dirt that rinses away. It's not surprising considering that the wool, silk, or cotton and the canvas has been around a little bit before you purchased them; they have traveled many miles, going from truck to truck and warehouse to warehouse; and how long have they been on those shelves in the store? When your canvas has dried, you will be so pleased to see all those colors, clean, clear, and fresh.

There are several devices that can be used for blocking. For small pieces, a cork memo board, marked off in inches, will do the trick nicely. If you're lucky enough to find a lace doily stretcher, every ¼ inch over the whole surface of the board has a small nail hole. All you have to do is stretch your canvas, using the guide lines you marked on your canvas to keep it straight, and put small nails through the canvas and into the holes of the stretcher.

For larger pieces, I like to use a piece of pressed wallboard, which any lumber yard will cut for you. Mark it off in inches, and you are ready to go. Then there is a commercial needlepoint blocking device which is adjustable to various sizes. It has little brass hooks on which you stretch your canvas. But unless you block a lot of canvases and have a lot of storage space, this can be a clumsy piece of equipment to store around the house. Nevertheless, I find it a very flexible tool.

If you don't want to bother with boards and stretching devices, find an old desk or table you don't care about, or even an old unused flush door, and tack the piece to that. As long as the surface isn't warped, use whatever is handy.

I have found ordinary thumb tacks untrustworthy. They have a tendency to pop out when the canvas is being stretched. I prefer push pins, or those long heavy-headed thumb tacks that artists use. It doesn't matter if they rust, the rust marks will be beyond the work on a part of the canvas that will never show.

With your wallboard or corkboard marked, and following the center marks on the edges of your canvas, start tacking and stretching from the centers of the canvas edges out to the corners, placing a tack every ½ inch. Some people advise blocking with the finished side of the piece facing the board. I don't know what difference it makes. Anyway it's a peculiar quirk of mine I guess, but I like to look at the piece as it dries. And I *don't* enjoy looking at the back of the piece! In about 24 to 36 hours the canvas will be dry, and you can pull out the tacks or nails.

This method of blocking may seem complicated and time-consuming to you, but just putting the piece on an ironing board and steaming it will never give you a truly blocked result. Consider this—the canvas, which is now between two layers of wool, the stitchery, must be thoroughly straightened and squared. It takes a lot of straightening to get through those three layers of fabric!

6. As in the "make-a-pillow, start-a-rug" project, the method I prefer for joining canvases is to leave a part of the border or edge incomplete and at least $1\frac{1}{2}$ inches of canvas on all sides. Overlap the two edges, making sure that the canvas squares, or meshes, line up, and match exactly, and that the threads are running the same way. Follow the selvage edges to be sure the weave is in the same direction. Baste the two canvases together, one on top of the other, matching the meshes. Then match your needlepoint stitchery, and stitch through the two canvases. When you have four corners meeting, it could be a little bulky. So you will have to miter very carefully to eliminate this, but it can be done. Mitering is cutting each edge of a join on an angle so that the pieces meet flush, rather than overlapping.

There is another method of joining that is especially good for smaller pieces and if you don't wish to do too much stitchery over double canvas. Now fold your canvas to the back, leaving only one row of meshes beyond the edge of your stitches. Miter the corners very carefully, then whip-stitch the folded-over canvas to the back. Cut off the binding hems, except for the very outer edges of a rug. Now match the folded edges together, doing a kind of zig-zag basting stitch so the meshes won't slip up or down. Finally, a row of tent stitch across the join will hold the edges together firmly.

Before proceeding with the above, each piece should be blocked first. And, to avoid confusion at this point, it might be a good idea to mark each piece, before beginning your joining, with an arrow on the sides that parallel the selvage line.

This is the method I used to patch the burnt hole in the tobacco leaf pillow in Chapter 1. I simply cut a small piece of 12-gauge penelope canvas and placed it under the burnt hole, making sure that the canvas squares lined up and matched and that the threads were running the correct way. I basted with sewing thread to keep the small piece securely in place and then began my needlepoint stitches, which went through two layers of canvas around the one layer patch of the actual burnt hole.

6. What is the best way to join canvases?

Opposite
Butterfly, half-cross stitch with triangle-stitch border.

7. How do you insert petit point into a larger-mesh canvas?

7. Inserting petit point into a larger-mesh canvas seems very simple. However, the procedure is tedious, and if your patience has a low threshold, don't try it. But once you've tried it, you'll use it more and more. The results are spectacular, and you can get such a variety in all your work. The underwater hippo (page 46) and the butterfly in the baby zebra were done this way (page 2).

First, mark the position and outline of the petit point on the larger-gauge canvas. This will serve as a guide if you should decide to do a little background before you have inserted the finer piece. When the petit point is completed, block at first. After it has dried completely, cut the hemmed edge away, leaving at least 3 inches of bare canvas from the outer edges of the stitchery. Start pulling the canvas threads away, unraveling toward the stitchery. As you get close to the petit point, be careful *not* to pull threads out of the stitchery.

Now you've got a mess of fringe on all sides. Be sure to be a bit extravagant with the fine canvas. If you cut too close to the stitches, it will be difficult to weave the short fringe into the larger canvas. Place it over the large canvas, lining it up with your outline. You can use a dot or two of Sobo or Elmer's Glue-all for added security, but use it sparingly as it has a tendency to harden. Now use some basting stitches to hold the canvases firmly together.

Then, with a very fine crochet hook or a blunt needle, weave each separated thread of the finer canvas in and out of the larger meshes, making sure that they all end up on the reverse side of the larger-mesh canvas. Work the background stitchery right up to and through the petit point. This will cover the woven raveled threads and blend into the petit point. Possibly you will have to use a few ad-lib stitches to complete the blending.

8. What are the best needles to use in doing needlepoint?

8. The needles you use for needlepoint should be blunt with a good, long eye and of good polish. It is useful to keep one of those pumice or graphite strawberries with your work to keep your needle smooth. The sizes of needlepoint needles range from 24 to 14—the larger the number, the smaller the needle.

80

So, for 5-point canvas and rug yarn, you should use a 14 or 16 needle. As the gauge of your canvas increases and your yarns are finer, use a higher-numbered needle. I prefer a slightly larger needle than what is usually recommended, because I find it easier to work with, and it lessens the risk of puncturing the canvas threads.

9. How do I hold my canvas? With my hands! Seriously, I don't think there can be a rule or a magic instruction about how to hold the canvas while working. It is a matter of personal comfort. Sometimes when working fine petit point, I use a pair of embroidery hoops to keep the delicate canvas firm.

9. How do you hold your canvas when working?

10. Obviously, I would never use watercolor paints on a canvas. The colors would run in blocking, and they would be very difficult to wash out. I always use acrylic paints because of their flexibility and quick-drying quality. I even use them for all my original sketches. I rarely paint the canvas, because I feel more freedom working from the sketch. I only transfer the outlines for guidance. However, if it is awkward for me to drag the sketch around from place to place, I might paint some areas very thinly, but a slightly different shade from the yarns. It is very difficult to see your progress if you match your yarns exactly to the color of the painting on the canvas.

10. Do you paint on canvas with watercolors?

Tight stitching pulls a canvas out of line. Notice how distorted the marked square on the upper left is, and how the once-straight threads have been pulled out of line.

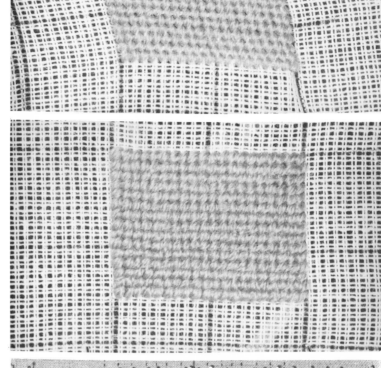

Keep the stitching puffy and loose. Then the piece is almost completely in line, even though it has not been blocked.

A well-prepared canvas can be easily blocked back into shape. The lines drawn through the center horizontally and vertically are lined up, and the hemmed edges provide a firm edge for tacking to the blocking board.

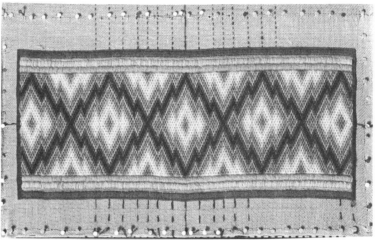

Blocking on a cork board with push pins.

82

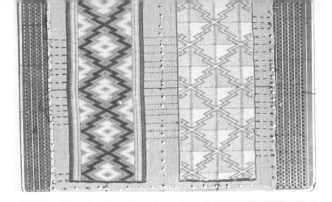

If you are lucky enough to find a lace-doily stretcher, it is a perfect aid in blocking, since it has holes lined up every $\frac{1}{4}$-inch over the surface for nails.

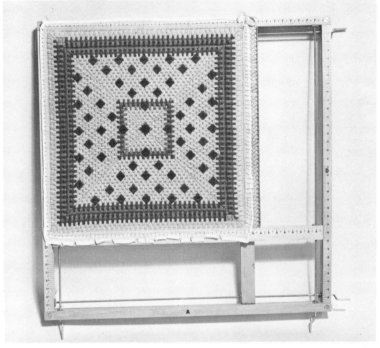

This is called a needlepoint blocking device (courtesy of Meyer Enterprises, Inc., P.O. Box 644, Sharon, Pa. 16146). It is marked in inches, and has hooks and a tension system.

Joining canvases, method 1. Overlap the meshes, one canvas on top of the other, and whip-stitch them together with sewing thread. Make sure all the meshes match perfectly.

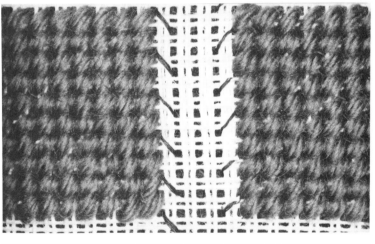

Back of the joined canvases. I always suggest overlapping about an inch when joining this way; these samples were done on 5-point penelope in diagonal tent stitch.

83

After joining, make your stitches through both layers of canvas.

Joining canvases, method 2. Join front of the work with sewing thread in double whip stitch, so that the meshes match perfectly and there is one row only between the two pieces of needlepoint. The excess canvas on each edge has been folded back, as in the usual seam sewing.

Back of the work, showing canvases folded back and secured with double whip stitch.

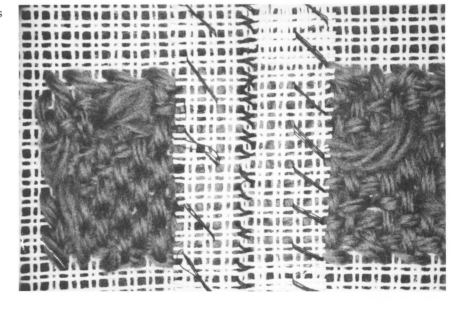

After joining, make one row of stitches across the edge. This method makes it unnecessary to sew through two layers of canvas.

Patching damaged canvas. To repair canvas, match at least 6 meshes beyond the hole by overlapping canvas. Carefully baste the two pieces together, and then stitch over them both. This is 10-point penelope in which a hole was accidentally burned.

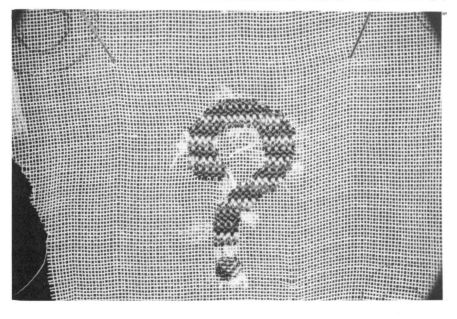

Inserting petit point in a larger-gauge canvas. This is the petit point on 28-point mono canvas. It would take a long time to complete the background with such fine meshes, so only the design is worked on this canvas. The background will be 10-point mono.

First, threads around the petit point are unraveled, taking care not to pull them out through the stitching.

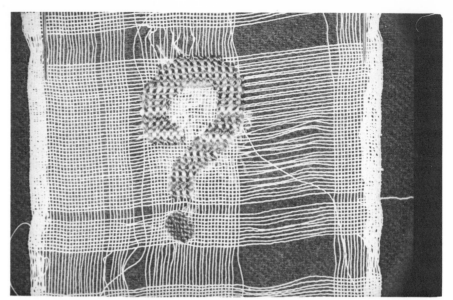

When unraveling is completed, the piece is ready for insertion.

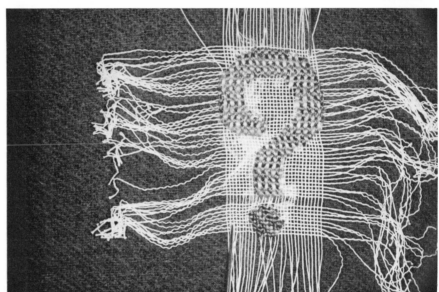

The larger-gauge canvas is marked where the petit point is to be inserted.

86

Insertion is pinned into place, right over markings. It can be basted for added security.

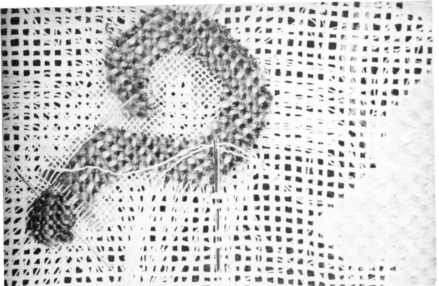

Loose ends of the petit-point canvas in brick stitch are threaded through a needle, and woven in and out of the larger canvas for at least $\frac{1}{2}$ inch —probably 1 inch would be better. To avoid a sharp line or heavy bump in the final stitching, these threads are woven into the larger canvas somewhat unevenly.

Insertion is completed by stitching right up to the edge of the petit point with the background stitch, also brick stitch, and then blending the stitches into the petit point with ad-lib stitches.

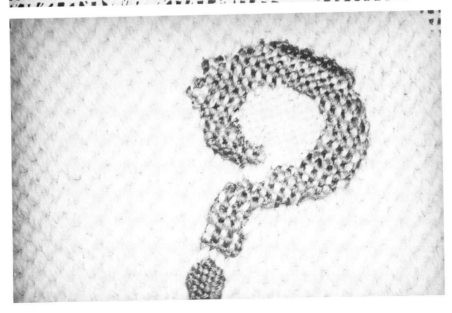

Project 1 (page 70)

Proof of the durability of acrylic paints and top quality wools, silks, and canvas is an incident that happened to me while I was playing in Washington, D.C., in *She Stoops to Conquer* at Ford's Theatre. I was actually the first star to appear there since President Lincoln was shot. I must say, it was rather spooky trying to play a comedy with that gaping empty box draped in flags.

After playing a matinee, I stopped off at a supermarket to pick up some food for my dogs. My attention wandered for a moment. (I learned a lesson then, never again to be so fascinated by an unfamiliar wine label.) The next thing I knew my purse had been snatched. I cannot remember when it was so difficult for me to utter a sound. I stood there with my mouth making motions, like a goldfish out of water, soundless!

Finally, something came out of my throat. "My purse! My purse!" There was pandemonium in the market. At last a policeman appeared. His first question was, "How old are you?"

"How old do I have to be to have my purse snatched?" I shot back at him. Then he wanted to know the contents of my purse. Good heavens! Contents! Well, the money didn't matter. But there were all my credit cards, driver's license, a recently repaired double string of beautiful pearls, two beautiful large gold medals that I always carried with me. They were gifts of my dear friend, the late Don Loper—a Saint Francis and a Saint Genesius, patron saint of actors.

But worst of all, there was an almost completed petit-point portrait of a monkey, with the original sketch and all the silks. Just how do you explain to a hulking policeman what a piece of petit point is?

Several nights later, during a performance, we heard the news that Dr. Martin Luther King had been shot. The next day the city was in a terrible state, looting, fires, curfews, police, and soldiers all over the place. With the police so occupied, I hadn't a hope of ever seeing my purse again. The theatre was closed and boarded up, because technically it is designated as a national museum and is government property.

After about a week, we reopened, and the city seemed to return to normal. But the boarded-up and burned-out shops were a ghastly reminder of those dreadful days. I had almost forgotten about the purse.

88

About a month later, I received a call from a state police trooper in a small town in Maryland. He asked me to come and identify the purse. I couldn't believe it! I called a friend of mine, and we drove to the tiny town and to the tiny police station. There was my purse, dripping wet, on the counter. It was more than a puzzlement. My empty wallet, my son's picture, the credit cards, and my driver's license were all bone dry. Of course, gone were the pearls, the medals, the sketch, and the petit-point monkey. Well, I knew then I would never attempt to do that monkey again!

The trooper asked if I would like to see where the purse was found. Not me! "What was the point?" I thought. But my friend had a fiendish curiousity. So we followed the trooper over the muddy, narrow road along the bank of the Potomac River. He stopped at a most unlikely and dismal spot. There was barely any road at all. The ground was muddy and sloshy.

We began to look around. Yich! "Why bother?" I thought. Suddenly my friend bent down and pulled a wadded mess out of the mud. It was only recognizable to me—a whole bunch of my silks, hopelessly tangled. A little farther along, there was the sketch. And then, muddy, filthy, and soaked—my monkey. I almost cried at the horrible sight of it. Perhaps it would have been better never to have found it at all.

Salvaging any of it was surely hopeless. That night in my apartment after the performance, I looked at the muddy mess I had left on the table. All that work! All that time! I brushed some dried mud off the sketch. Fortunately I had backed the paper with heavy masking tape. The colors weren't too bad, a little faded, but enough for me to work.

I looked at the unfinished canvas. I thought, "What's to lose?" It was a mess anyway. So I dumped it into a basin, and washed it thoroughly. I rinsed it several times and blocked it. Then I turned my back on it and went to bed.

The next morning the monkey was dry, bright and shining, and staring at me. The eyes seemed to challenge me to finish it. I did finish it—that afternoon—and then reblocked it. If that experience isn't a testimonial to acrylic paints and quality materials, I don't know what is!

Nothing could ever make me part with that monkey. It is on 18-point penelope canvas, splitting the threads to make it 36-point for the head and chest of the monkey. The background is in reverse half-cross stitch (see page 39).

6
Do You Frame Yourself? How Do You Mount Pictures, Bags, Pillows, and Covered Objects?

We are now approaching opening night, or the finish line, or that gift deadline, and it's terrifying. Your stitchery is completed, the piece is blocked and has dried. It looks beautiful. But face reality—after all that work, it isn't finished yet. It is not ready for opening night, for critical and audience acceptance. There are some painful decisions to make, and steps to take, before your work is presentable—for an early closing or a long, long run!

Questions and Answers

1. In all honesty, I do not *know* the *best* way to mount a needlepoint bag. So much depends on the style of the purse and your own sewing ability, either by hand or machine. If it is a simple one-piece clutch purse, there is no problem: The lining follows the template of the needlepoint, and can be done by hand or machine.

But if it's more than one piece, and you want it leather-lined, or fabric-lined, with inside pockets and a handsome frame, please go to strangers. It will be costly but very well worth it. For the proper result, have a professional do it. They have the proper materials and machines to produce a fine result. And they will, as a rule, treat your work with care and respect.

2. I rarely frame pieces myself, especially if they are large. They should be handled like a painting on canvas. After blocking, the needlepoint can be stapled to stretchers, which can be purchased in any art supply store, in all dimensions. Then I advise you to consult with a framer whose taste and ability you trust. Have a consultation and choose the color, style, frame, matting, and mounting that is most suitable for your piece.

Prowling around antique shops and even "junque" shops, I try to have a supply of old and usable frames on hand, so that when I design and stitch, I usually have a particular frame in mind that suits the subject and the design. Sometimes I forget, and get carried away by the design and the stitchery, making it the wrong size for any of my frames. Then I have to resort to custom work, as in the case of the baby zebra and the mustard seed parable.

When I was working on the portrait of the lost monkey that was later found, I had a definite frame in mind and on hand.

1. What is the best way to mount a needlepoint bag?

2. How do you frame your needlepoint pictures?

The portrait was designed to suit it. In fact, I think they complement each other very well. Fortunately, the frame still had its original oval backing, so it was simple to cut the canvas, leaving about a ½ inch of canvas around the monkey. Before applying the piece to the backing, I put a bit of cotton batting on the back of the canvas to give it a little roundness and more dimension. Then I folded the canvas back and glued it to the oval cardboard.

The costume I wore as Mrs. Hardcastle in *She Stoops to Conquer* was huge with overskirts on top of many underskirts. And it was the most beautiful shade of bronze green. I cut enough fabric out of the enormous hem to cover the backing piece and the front mat, and then assembled it all in the frame (see page 70).

I do *not* like glass covering needlepoint, not even non-reflecting glass. It gives the stitchery a very dead, flat appearance. It is wonderful to be able to get close to the stitchery and even touch it. For instance, I have had two pieces hanging in my kitchen for several years. There is no glass covering them. There is no greasiness on the stitchery, and the colors are like new. They are surviving just fine—which leads directly to the answer of the next question on care of needlepoint pieces.

3. How do you care for your pieces after they have been made into pillows and pictures?

3. As soon as any piece has dried after blocking, I spray it with Scotchgard, a fabric protector. It does help a great deal to retard stains. Vacuuming pillows and the fronts and backs of framed pieces will keep them looking lively and clean. Usually I don't like to cover the backs of large framed canvases with paper. I think they need to breathe. Also a bit of spray starch on the back of your canvas will retard the settling of dirt and dust into the stitchery.

No piece of needlepoint ever made was or will be exposed to more dirt and grime than the two pieces Joanne Woodward and I were working on while on location in the underground station in London during the filming of *Summer Wishes, Winter Dreams*. If I remember correctly, Joanne was working on a very pastel, softly shaded piece, and I was working on the well-traveled baby zebra. It occurred to me while working with Joanne—whether needlepointing, rehearsing or filming—that she and her husband Paul Newman (who doesn't do needlepoint) are a combine of such physical beauty and enormous talent that that it's almost illegal and plainly unfair to us poor plebians! After proper washing and blocking, the baby zebra is bright and shiny, as you can see on page 2.

4. As with framing, custom work and labor for pillows is very costly these days. And since I am very clumsy with the sewing machine, I usually leave the pillow work to the experts. However, whenever I am shopping and happen to find well-made, ready-made pillows, I grab them. Then I adjust my designs to their dimensions. I did this with the two narrow bargello designs (see page 23). I cut the canvas to about 1 inch from the edge of the stitchery, mitered the corners, folded back the canvas, and whip-stitched the last row of stitchery into the binding of the ready-made pillows.

You may not think this method produces the greatest looking result, but it does have one advantage: You can enjoy the pillow, or the "giftee" can enjoy it, until such time when you feel extravagant. Then you can rip the canvas off the ready-made pillow with ease, and take it to a good upholsterer to have it done professionally. But that's only when your purse is bulging!

4. How do you execute pillows, wastebaskets, pencil holders, tissue-box covers, and doorstops?

93

Project 1

Buy a straight-sided wastebasket, round, oval, or square. It must have the same dimensions at the top and bottom, and of course your stitchery must be exactly as high as the basket. Make one piece just wide enough to go all around the basket. The finishing is simple. I do it two ways. First, after blocking is completed, fold back the canvas on all four sides, right to the edges of the work. A few drops of Elmer's or Sobo glue strategically placed around the wastebasket will help for added security. Then whip-stitch the two edges together at the side or back of the wastebasket. If your needlepoint stitchery and design match, this seam will barely show.

The other method is equally as simple. After washing and rolling the canvas in a towel, stretch it right onto the wastebasket. Use heavy masking tape whenever needed to keep it secure and in place. Now stitch the two joining edges together. It will be a little slithery because of the wetness, but by the time it has dried, it will be very tight around the wastebasket. It may need a few correctional stitches here and there. These same two methods can be used for any cylindrical base you may choose, such as a lamp base perhaps, or on juice cans of all sizes for pencil holders, toothbrush holders, or whatever purpose you choose (see page 47).

Covering cylindrical forms with needlepoint is easy to do. See directions in Project 1. Here a wastepaper basket is matched by a small vase or pencil holder, actually a covered juice can.

94

Project 2

Facial-tissue boxes and doorstops are essentially the same forms. Once you have found the formula or procedure that works best for you, the variations are endless. First of all, no matter what the size, save a few empty facial-tissue boxes just to have on hand in case you have to make a quick gift.

Open the empty box carefully at the four corners, removing the bottom. When flattened out, it becomes the template for your design on the canvas. After marking your canvas centers, place the opened cardboard box on the canvas, matching the centers, and draw the outline around the template. Mark the opening for the tissues. Allow for at least two extra rows of stitchery on all sides because the needlework will have to be just a little larger than the box size you have chosen. It will eventually have to slip *over* another box of tissues.

After blocking (don't cut the center tissue opening before blocking—it makes for twice the work), I cut the side and end panels away from the original box that I used as a pattern, leaving only the top of the box. I glue this to the back of the canvas, matching the openings for the tissues. This makes a perfect guide for cutting the opening in the canvas. Cut through the center of the unworked canvas, making slight angle slashes at the corners. Turn back the unworked canvas and glue the edges to the cardboard box top.

If you wish to make the cover very elegant, you can line the back of the canvas with a bit of fancy material. Then sew the canvas into its box shape by hand or machine, so it can slip on and off. Just remember to leave the short corner seams for the last. It's much easier to handle that way. Once you have done one of these, all box shapes will be easy for you (see page 47).

96

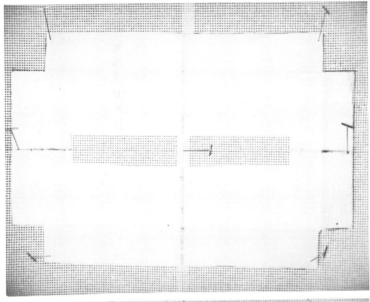

To make a template for a tissue-box cover, remove the bottom of an empty box, flatten out the rest, and mark the center with horizontal and vertical lines. Then place the template on a marked canvas, matching centers.

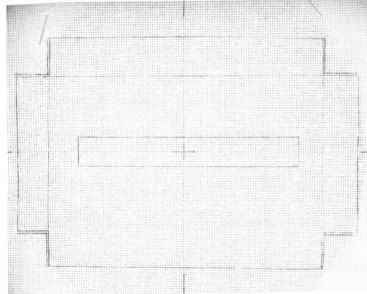

Draw around the pattern, keeping center opening smaller than actual box opening, to allow for small turn under when work is finished. Also allow 2 or 3 extra meshes all around the edges, for the same reason.

Questions, questions, questions!

I hope the answers to the questions I have been asked over the years have provided you with a new perspective in needlepoint. And I am hopeful that the answers have been helpful in solving some of your stitchery problems, and that you've had a little fun along the way.

If I haven't answered *your* questions, please write to me in care of Van Nostrand Reinhold Company, 450 West 33 Street, New York, New York 10001.

7
Stitches

Some people, in giving instructions for needlepoint, count the number of threads over which a stitch is done. I go by meshes —the holes in the canvas. As you can easily see in the illustrations, when inserting the needle, I count the meshes from the mesh where the yarn came through the canvas to the front, and when bringing out the needle, I count from the mesh where the yarn went through to the back.

When you are finished with one row, you turn the canvas around and follow the directions as before.

In my first book, I presented the slanting stitches, then the straight stitches, and finally herringbone and fringe, which didn't fit into either category. In the following pages, I have presented the stitches in the order they are mentioned in the text—not necessarily from easiest to hardest—so that you can find them while reading through the questions, answers, and projects. They can also be found in the Index of Stitches at the back of the book.

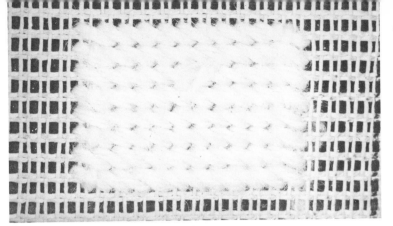

Stitches in Chapter 1

TENT STITCH

Tent stitch, *back view.* Completed stitch is shown on page 21.

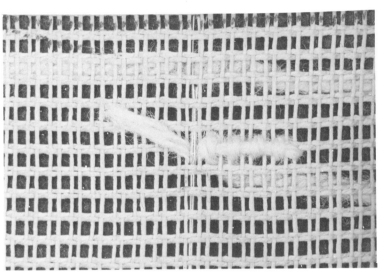

Back tuck-in, *for beginning all stitches, including tent stitch.* Always start with a neat tuck-in at the back of the canvas. Leave at least an inch of yarn at the back. Hold it there with one hand and make sure the needle covers it as you draw through to the front for 5 or 6 stitches. Once work is under way, you can simply weave ends into the back of the stitches or row before. This holds for ending a strand of yarn, too.

Tent stitch, *step 1.* Starting at the right, bring needle through to front of canvas. Insert it 1 mesh above and 1 mesh to right; bring it out 1 mesh below and 2 meshes to left.

Tent stitch, *step 2.* Again insert needle 1 mesh above and 1 mesh to right; bring it out 1 mesh below and 2 meshes to left. Continue to end of row.

99

Tent stitch, *step 3.* Insert needle 1 mesh above and 1 mesh to right; bring it out 1 mesh directly below. You are now ready to start row 2.

Tent stitch, *step 1, row 2.* Turn the work around and continue as in step 2. (Illustration shows position of needle before turning work.)

STRAIGHT CASHMERE STITCH

Straight cashmere stitch. This stitch resembles Scotch stitch or an elongated mosaic stitch, and the techniques are very similar (see page 21 for completed stitch). It is worked over a rectangle 3 meshes high and 2 meshes wide, which can be marked on the canvas, and can be done either from right or left.

Step 1. Bring the needle to front of canvas 1 mesh below (as if to make a tent or half-cross stitch). Insert it 1 mesh above and 1 mesh to right. Bring it to front of canvas 1 mesh below and 2 meshes to left.

Straight cashmere stitch, *step 2.* Insert needle 2 meshes above and 2 meshes to the right. Bring needle out 1 mesh below and 2 meshes to left.

100

Straight cashmere stitch, *step 3.* Insert needle 2 meshes above and 2 meshes to right. Bring needle to front 1 mesh below and 2 meshes to left.

Straight cashmere stitch, *step 4.* Insert needle 1 mesh above and 1 mesh to right. Bring it out 3 meshes down and 2 meshes to left. To continue, bring needle up 1 mesh and follow from step 1.

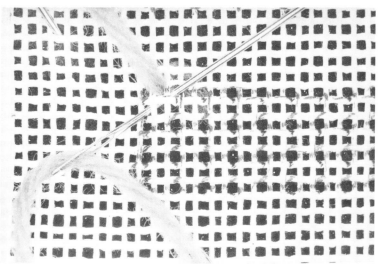

HORIZONTAL MOSAIC STITCH

Horizontal mosaic stitch *(see page 21), step 1.* Starting at the left, bring needle through to front of canvas. Insert it 1 mesh below and 1 mesh to the left; bring it out 1 mesh above and 2 meshes to the right.

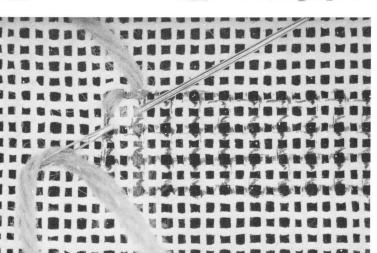

Horizontal mosaic stitch, *step 2.* Insert needle 2 meshes below and 2 meshes to the left; bring it out 1 mesh above and 2 meshes to the right.

101

Horizontal mosaic stitch, *step 3.* Insert needle 1 mesh below and 1 mesh to the left; bring it out 2 meshes above and 2 meshes to the right.

Horizontal mosaic stitch, *step 4.* To continue, repeat from step 1.

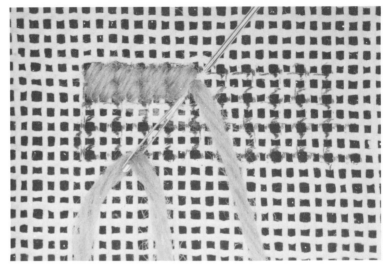

TWO-STEP HERRINGBONE STITCH

Two-step herringbone *(see pages 21 and 64), step 1, row 1.* Bring needle through to the front 5 meshes below the top line of the row. Insert it 5 meshes above and 2 meshes to the right; bring it out 1 mesh to the left.

Two-step herringbone, *step 2.* Insert needle 5 meshes below and 2 meshes to the right; bring it out 1 mesh to the left.

102

Two-step herringbone, *to continue Color 1.* Repeat steps 1 and 2.

Two-step herringbone, *step 1, Color 2.* Bring needle to the front 5 meshes above bottom row, 1 mesh to the left of previous stitch. Insert needle 5 meshes below and 2 meshes to the right; bring it to the front 1 mesh to the left.

Two-step herringbone, *step 2.* Insert needle 5 meshes above and 2 meshes to the right; bring it to the front 1 mesh to the left. Continue across the row by repeating steps 1 and 2.

Two-step herringbone, *2 rows of completed stitch.* Herringbone may be done in 3, 4, 5, or 6 steps (see page 64) by varying the number of meshes that are skipped between each stitch and the starting places for each color.

103

KNOTTED STITCH

Knotted stitch. My version of the knotted stitch is a bit unorthodox, and is done over 5 meshes instead of the conventional 3 (see page 28 for completed stitch). But I think this version has more definition and covers more canvas quickly.

Step 1. Bring needle to the front 5 meshes below the top of the row. Insert needle 5 meshes above and 1 mesh to the right; bring it out 3 meshes down.

Knotted stitch, *step 2.* Insert needle 1 mesh above and 1 mesh to the left. This makes a small tent stitch across a slanting Gobelin. Bring needle out 3 meshes below and 1 mesh to the right.

Knotted stitch, *step 3.* Insert needle 5 meshes above and 1 mesh to the right. Continue across the row and end yarn. Although this stitch can be worked back and forth like other stitches, I think it looks neater when worked always from the same direction.

Knotted stitch, *step 1, row 2.* From now on all rows are started 4 meshes below the last row, but the needle is inserted 5 meshes up, thus overlapping the rows.

104

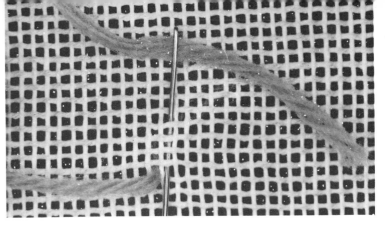

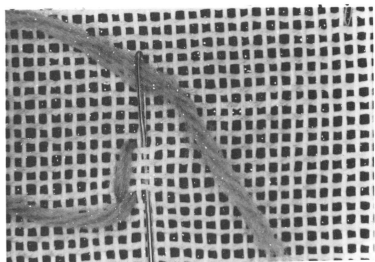

SLANTING GOBELIN STITCH

Slanting Gobelin stitch, *(see page 28 for completed stitch)*, may sound like just another variation of the basic slanting stitch, but as you can see, it looks very different from the half-cross and tent stitches.

Step 1, row 1. Starting at the left, bring needle through to front of canvas a desired number of meshes below the edge (in the illustration, 4 meshes). Insert needle 4 meshes above and 1 mesh to right; bring it out 4 meshes directly below.

Slanting Gobelin stitch, *step 2.* Insert needle 4 meshes above and 1 mesh to right; bring it out 4 meshes directly below. Continue to end of row.

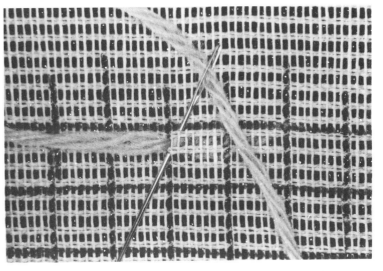

SCOTCH STITCH

Scotch stitch (see pages 28 and 66). The basic Scotch stitch can be done in squares of 3, 4, 5, or 6 meshes. If the squares are marked off as illustrated in the following pictures, no counting will be necessary once you begin. Scotch stitch can be done diagonally or horizontally: the basic square is the same for both.

Step 1. Starting at the left, bring needle through to front of canvas. Insert it 1 mesh above and 1 mesh to right; bring it out 2 meshes below and 1 mesh to left.

Scotch stitch, *step 2.* Insert needle 2 meshes above and 2 meshes to right; bring it out 3 meshes below and 2 meshes to left.

105

Scotch stitch, *step 3.* Insert needle 3 meshes above and 3 meshes to right; bring it out 4 meshes below and 3 meshes to left.

Scotch stitch, *step 4.* Insert needle 4 meshes above and 4 meshes to right; bring it out 4 meshes below and 3 meshes to left. For the next two stitches, insert needle 3 meshes above and 3 meshes to right; bring it out 3 meshes below and 2 meshes to left; then insert needle 2 meshes above and 2 meshes to right; bring it out 2 meshes below and 1 mesh to left.

Scotch stitch, *to continue horizontally.* Complete the basic square by inserting needle 1 mesh above and 1 mesh to right (as in step 5); bring it out 2 meshes directly above. Then insert needle 1 mesh above and 1 mesh to right; bring it out 2 meshes below and 1 mesh to left. continue from step 2 to complete square.

Scotch stitch, *to continue diagonally.* Complete the basic square by inserting needle 1 mesh above and 1 mesh to right (a tent stitch); bring it out 2 meshes directly below.

106

Scotch stitch, *diagonal, step* 2. Insert needle 1 mesh above and 1 mesh to right; bring it out 2 meshes below and 1 mesh to left. Continue from step 2 to complete square.

SIX-STEP HERRINGBONE STITCH

Six-step herringbone stitch. The illusion of depth created by shading or coloring in herringbone is very pleasing (see page 28). The stitch can be done in as many as six different colors. For purposes of illustration in black and white here, four shades of gray, from very light to charcoal, are used.

Herringbone works best on penelope. Marking the canvas is a great help: draw horizontal lines every 4 meshes, a vertical line 4 meshes to the right of the starting point, and vertical lines every 6 meshes after that, as in the following pictures. If you are doing a border or other small area, the ordinary method of tucking in will work perfectly well. However, if the area to be covered is large, don't tuck in at the beginning and end of each row, which makes the edges very bulky. Instead, weave the ends in and out for 5 or 6 meshes. *Herringbone must be worked from left to right.*

Row 1, Color 1: Starting at the left, bring needle through to front of canvas 4 meshes below top edge. Insert needle 1 mesh below and 1 mesh to right; bring it out 1 mesh directly to left.

107

Six-step herringbone stitch, *step 2.* Insert needle 4 meshes above and 4 meshes to right; bring it out 1 mesh directly to left.

Six-step herringbone, *step 3.* Insert needle 4 meshes below and 4 meshes to right; bring it out 1 mesh directly to left. To continue, repeat from step 2. To begin next row, proceed from step 3 as follows.

Six-step herringbone, *Row 2, Color 1 (or 2):* Bring needle through to front 3 meshes below top edge (1 mesh above first stitch in Row 1). Insert needle 2 meshes below and 2 meshes to right; bring it out 1 mesh directly to left.

Six-step herringbone, *step 2.* Insert needle 4 meshes above and 4 meshes to right (1 mesh to right of second stitch in Row 1); bring it out 1 mesh directly to left. Continue as in step 3 of Row 1.

Six-step herringbone, *Row 3, Color 2 (or 3):* Bring needle through to front 1 mesh below top edge (1 mesh above first stitch in Row 2). Insert needle 3 meshes below and 3 meshes to right; bring it out 1 mesh directly to left.

Six-step herringbone, *step 2.* Insert needle 4 meshes above and 4 meshes to right (1 mesh to right of second stitch in Row 2); bring it out 1 mesh directly to left. Continue as in step 3 of Row 1.

Six-step herringbone, *Row 4, Color 2 (or 4):* Bring needle through to front through top mesh. Insert it 4 meshes below and 4 meshes to right; bring it out 1 mesh directly to left.

Six-step herringbone, *step 2.* Insert needle 4 meshes above and 4 meshes to right (1 mesh to right of second stitch in Row 3), bring it out 1 mesh directly to left. Continue as in step 3 of Row 1.

109

Six-step herringbone, *Row 5, Color 3 (or 5):* Go carefully here. Bring needle through to front 4 meshes below top edge. Insert it 4 meshes above and 2 meshes to right (2 meshes to right of first stitch in Row 4); bring it out 1 mesh directly to left.

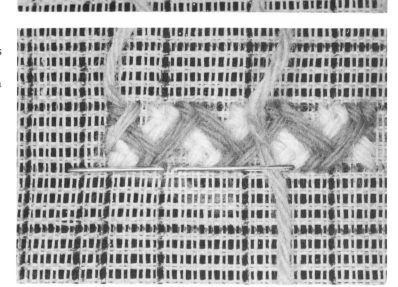

Six-step herringbone, *step 2.* Insert needle 4 meshes below and 4 meshes to right (1 mesh to right of second stitch in Row 4); bring it out 1 mesh directly to left. Continue as in step 2 of Row 1.

Six-step herringbone, *Row 6, Color 4 (or 6):* Bring needle through to front 5 meshes below top edge. Insert it 4 meshes above and 3 meshes to right (1 mesh to right of first stitch in Row 5); bring it out 1 mesh directly to left.

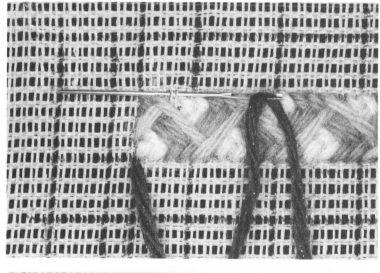

Six-step herringbone, *step 2.* Insert needle 4 meshes below and 4 meshes to right (1 mesh to right of second stitch in Row 5—the only place you *can* put it!); bring it out 1 mesh directly to left. Continue as in step 2 of Row 1.

110

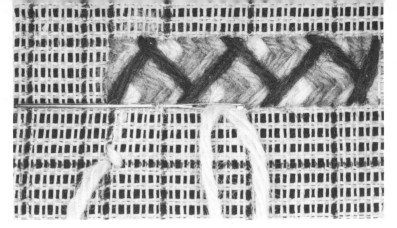

Six-step herringbone, *Rows 7-12:* Repeat the first six rows.

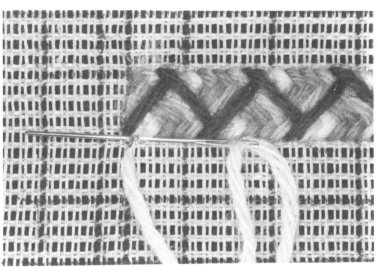

Six-step herringbone 2, (see page 28). This is worked exactly like regular herringbone for the first six rows. It is at the seventh row that the directions change.

Row 7, Color 1: Starting at the left, bring needle through to front of canvas 3 meshes above bottom edge (1 mesh below completed band). Insert needle 1 mesh above and 1 mesh to right; bring it out 1 mesh directly to left.

Six-step herringbone 2, *step 2.* Insert needle 4 meshes below and 4 meshes to right; bring it out 1 mesh directly to left.

Six-step herringbone 2, *step 3.* Insert needle 4 meshes above and 4 meshes to right; bring it out 1 mesh directly to left. To continue, repeat from step 2. To begin next row, proceed from step 3 as follows.

111

Six-step herringbone 2, *Row 8, Color 1 (or 2):* Bring needle through to front 2 meshes above bottom edge (1 mesh below first stitch in Row 7). Insert needle 2 meshes above and 2 meshes to right; bring it out 1 mesh directly to left. Continue as in step 2 of Row 7.

Six-step herringbone 2, *Row 9, Color 2 (or 3):* Bring needle through to front 1 mesh above bottom edge (1 mesh below first stitch in Row 8). Insert needle 3 meshes above and 3 meshes to right; bring it out 1 mesh directly to left. Continue as in step 2 of Row 7.

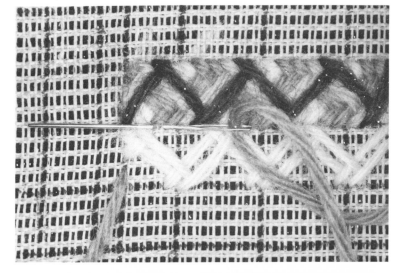

Six-step herringbone 2, *Row 10, Color 2 (or 4):* Bring needle through to front through bottom mesh. Insert it 4 meshes above and 4 meshes to right; bring it out 1 mesh directly to left. Continue as in step 2 of Row 7.

Six-step herringbone 2, *Row 11, Color 3 (or 5):* Bring needle through to front 3 meshes above bottom edge (1 mesh below first stitch in Row 7). Insert needle 3 meshes below and 2 meshes to right; bring it out 1 mesh directly to left. Continue as in step 3 of Row 7.

112

Six-step herringbone 2, *Row 12, Color 4 (or 6):* Bring needle through to front through 4 meshes above bottom edge (the same mesh as first stitch in Row 6). Insert needle 4 meshes below and 3 meshes to right; bring it out 1 mesh directly to left. Continue as in step 3 of Row 7.

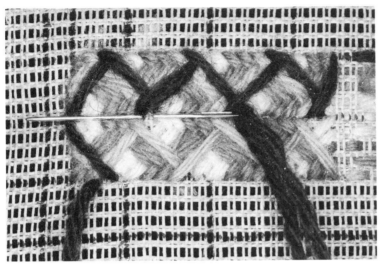

Six-step herringbone 2, *step 2.* Continue as before. The next stitch should meet the point of row 6, completing the diamond pattern.

FRINGE

Fringe. There are a variety of ways to handle fringe, depending on the effect you want. See page 29 for a completed wool fringe with cut loops. The length of a fringe is a matter of choice. For an average-size pillow (about 12 by 14 inches), I like the loops at least an inch long. The fringe given in the following pictures is very firm, and the knotting is not bulky. *You must work fringe from left to right.* It is easier to work from the bottom up; otherwise, the loops from the row above can get in your way. The number of rows and meshes between rows is a matter of choice: It depends on how full or scanty you want the fringe.

Step 1. Starting at the left, with needle and yarn in front of the canvas, insert needle and bring it out 1 mesh directly below.

113

Fringe, *step 2.* Holding the end of yarn down with left thumb, insert 1 mesh above (the same mesh as first insertion); bring it out 1 mesh to left. Pull it firmly to secure the yarn.

Fringe, *step 3.* Insert needle 1 mesh to right (again the same mesh as first insertion); bring it out 1 mesh below, leaving a loop of the desired length (I use my left thumb for measuring as I go along). Hold the loop in place with your thumb.

Fringe, *step 4.* Insert needle 1 mesh to right; bring it out 1 mesh to left. Pull this top stitch firmly but not too tightly. (If you are working on mono-canvas, insert needle 2 meshes to right and bring it out 2 meshes to left.)

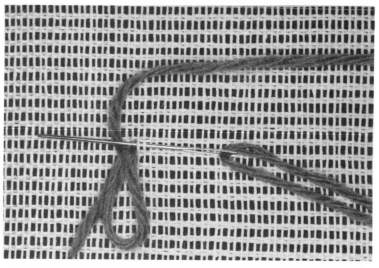

Fringe, *to continue.* Repeat from step 3.

114

Fringe, *row 2.* Again starting at the left, repeat from step 1.

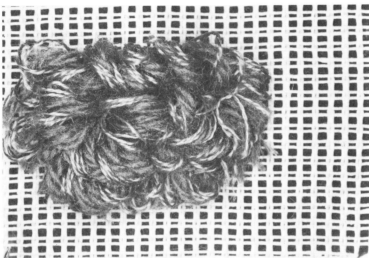

Shown here is a fringe of silk and wool with uncut loops.

BRICK STITCH

Brick stitch. I prefer this method of working brick stitch because it gives more backing (see page 33). Back view shown here.

Brick stitch, *step 1, row 1.* Starting at the left, bring needle through to front of canvas 2 meshes below the edge. Insert needle 2 meshes directly above; bring it out 2 meshes below and 2 meshes to right. Continue to end of row.

Brick stitch, *step 2.* Insert needle 2 meshes directly above; bring it out 3 meshes below and 1 mesh to left.

Brick stitch, *step 1, row 2.* Insert needle 2 meshes directly above; bring it out 2 meshes below and 2 meshes to left.

Brick stitch, *step 2.* Continue to end of row as before.

116

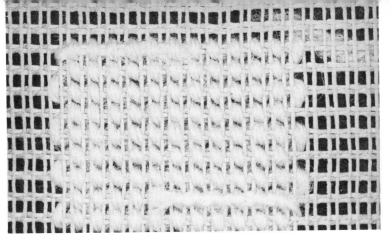

Stitches in Chapter 2

HALF-CROSS STITCH

Half-cross stitch, back view. This stitch cannot be done on mono canvas. Completed stitch shown on page 39

Half-cross stitch, *step 1.* Starting at the right, bring needle through to front of canvas. (Don't forget to hold the end of the strand in back for the tuck-in.) Insert needle 1 mesh above and 1 mesh to left; bring it out vertically, 1 mesh directly below. Don't pull the strand too tight— keep it relaxed and puffy.

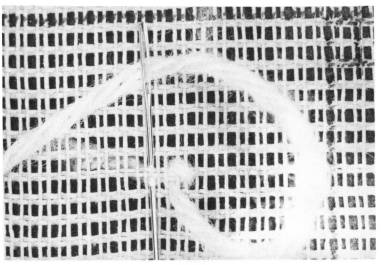

Half-cross stitch, *step 2.* Now, once again, insert needle 1 mesh above and 1 mesh to left; bring it out 1 mesh directly below. Continue to end of row.

Half-cross stitch, *step 1, row 2.* Simply turn the work around and continue as above. (Illustration shows position of needle before turning work.)

117

Half-cross stitch, *step 1, row 3.* Turn the canvas around again and continue. (Illustration shows position of needle after turning work.)

DIAGONAL TENT STITCH

Diagonal tent stitch. This looks a little frightening, but once you get the rhythm, it works quickly. One advantage of the stitch is that it holds its shape well (see page 42). *You must start this stitch at the upper right corner.*

Step 1. This begins just like the tent stitch. Starting at the right, bring needle through to front of canvas. Insert it 1 mesh above and 1 mesh to right; bring it out 1 mesh below and 2 meshes to left. Now, go carefully.

Diagonal tent stitch, *step 2.* Insert needle 1 mesh above and 1 mesh to right; bring it out vertically, 2 meshes directly below.

Diagonal tent stitch, *step 3.* Insert needle 1 mesh above and 1 mesh to right; bring it out 2 meshes below and 1 mesh to left.

118

Diagonal tent stitch, *step 4.* Insert needle 1 mesh above and 1 mesh to right; bring it out horizontally, 2 meshes directly to left.

Diagonal tent stitch, *step 5.* Insert needle 1 mesh above and 1 mesh to right; bring it out horizontally, 2 meshes directly to left.

Diagonal tent stitch, *step 6.* Insert needle 1 mesh above and 1 mesh to right; bring it out 1 mesh below and 2 meshes to left.

Diagonal tent stitch, *step 7.* Insert needle 1 mesh above and 1 mesh to right; bring it out vertically, 2 meshes directly below.

Diagonal tent stitch, *continuing downward diagonals.* When you are working down, the needle is vertical, except for the last stitch, when it is slanted (as in step 3).

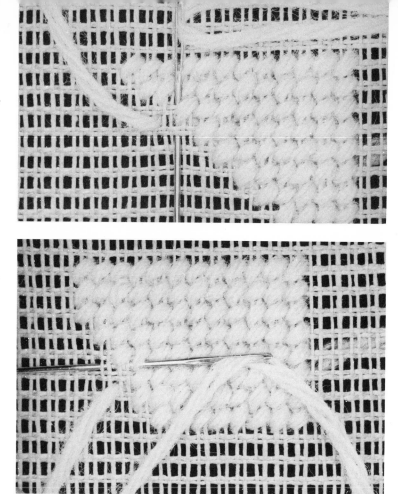

Diagonal tent stitch, *continuing upward diagonals.* When you are working up, the needle is horizontal, except for the last stitch, when it is slanted (as in step 6).

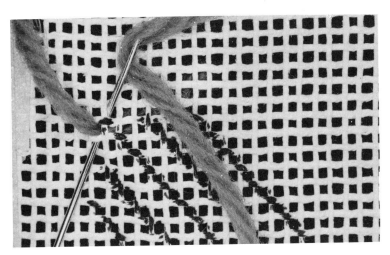

DIAGONAL MOSAIC STITCH
Diagonal mosaic stitch. This stitch has an easier rhythm than the horizontal mosaic stitch. It is lovely done in two or three different shades. Completed stitch in a single shade is shown on page 54. Mark off the working area as illustrated in the following pictures.

Step 1. Starting at left, bring needle through to front of canvas. Insert it 1 mesh above and 1 mesh to right; bring it out 2 meshes below and 1 mesh to left.

Diagonal mosaic stitch, *step 2.* Insert needle 2 meshes above and 2 meshes to right; bring it out 2 meshes below and 1 mesh to left.

Diagonal mosaic stitch, *step 3.* Insert needle 1 mesh above and 1 mesh to right; bring it out 2 meshes below and 1 mesh to left. To continue, repeat from step 2. To begin next row, proceed from step 2 as follows.

121

Diagonal mosaic stitch, *step 4.* Insert needle as in step 3; bring it out 1 mesh below and 3 meshes to left. To fill in space left between rows, insert needle 1 mesh above and 1 mesh to right; bring it out 1 mesh below and 2 meshes to left (a tent stitch). Row 2: insert needle 1 mesh above and 1 mesh to right; bring it out 1 mesh below and 2 meshes to left. Insert needle 2 meshes above and 2 meshes to right; bring it out 1 mesh below and 2 meshes to left. To continue, repeat these two stitches.

OBLIQUE STITCH

Oblique stitch. This covers well on both mono (see page 54) and penelope (shown here), and works quickly and simply.

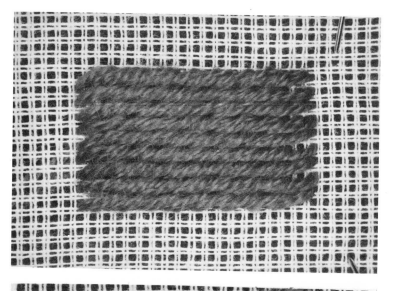

Oblique stitch, *step 1.* Starting at left, bring needle to the front. Insert needle 1 mesh above and 4 meshes to the right; bring it out 1 mesh below and 2 meshes to the left.

Oblique stitch, *step 2*. Continue across row. When row is complete, turn canvas, and repeat from step 1.

OLD FLORENTINE STITCH

Old Florentine stitch, (see page 57). If you mark off the canvas as illustrated in the following pictures, you will not need to count after the first few stitches.

Step 1. Starting at left, bring needle through to front 7 meshes below the edge. Insert needle 3 meshes directly above; bring it out 3 meshes below and 1 mesh to the right.

Old Florentine stitch, *step 2*. Insert needle 9 meshes directly above; bring it out 6 meshes below and 1 mesh to the right.

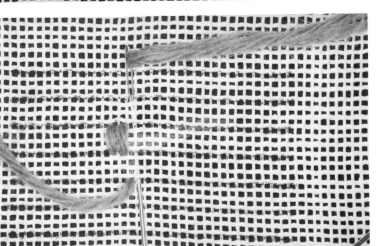

Old Florentine stitch, *step 3*. Insert needle 9 meshes directly above bring it out 9 meshes below and 1 mesh to right.

123

Old Florentine stitch, *step 4.* Insert needle 9 meshes directly above; bring it out 6 meshes below and 1 mesh to the right.

Old Florentine stitch, *step 5.* Insert needle 3 meshes directly above; bring it out 3 meshes below and 1 mesh to the right. To continue, repeat from step 2 to the end of row.

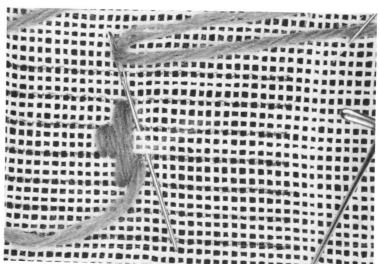

Old Florentine stitch, *step 6.* To begin next row, insert needle 3 meshes directly above; bring it out 9 meshes below and 2 meshes to the left.

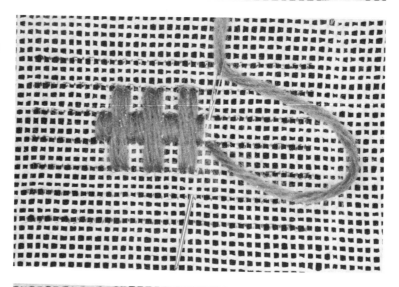

Old Florentine stitch, *step 1, row 2.* Insert needle 3 meshes directly above; bring it out 3 meshes below and 1 mesh to the left.

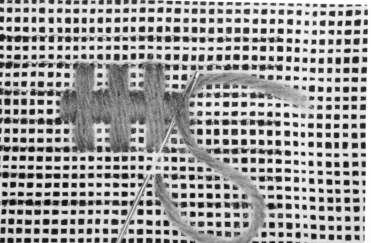

124

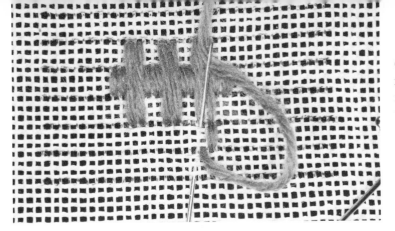

Old Florentine stitch, *step 2*. Insert needle 3 meshes directly above; bring it out 6 meshes below and 1 mesh to left. To continue, repeat from step 2, only working to the left.

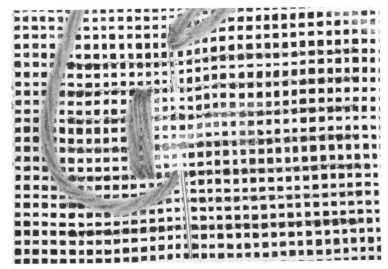

Old Florentine stitch, two-color variation, *step 1, Color 1*. Bring needle through to front of canvas 10 meshes below the edge. Insert needle 10 meshes directly above; bring it out 10 meshes below and 1 mesh to the right. Continue to end of row.

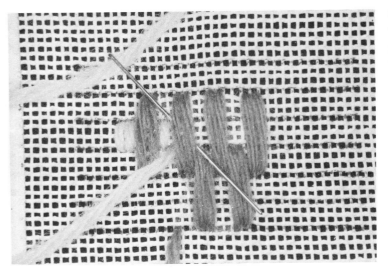

Old Florentine stitch, two-color variation, *step 1, Color 2*. Bring needle through to front of canvas 7 meshes below the edge and 2 meshes to left of first stitch in color 1. Insert needle 3 meshes directly above; bring it out 3 meshes below and 3 meshes to right. Continue to end of row.

Bibliography

Harbeson, Georgiana Brown. *American Needlework*. Santa Cruz, Calif: Bonanza, 1968.

DeDillmont, Therese. *Encyclopedia of Needlework*. Alsace, France: Mulhouse, n.d.

Hanley, Hope. *Needlepoint*. New York: Scribner's, 1964.

Ireys, Katherine. *Finishing and Mounting Your Needlepoint Pieces*. New York: Crowell, 1973.

Kaestner, Dorothy. *Four Way Bargello*. New York: Scribner's, 1972.

McGown, Pearl K. *Color in Hooked Rugs*. Sturbridge, Mass.: Lincoln House, 1954.

Russell, Pat. *Lettering for Embroidery*. New York: Van Nostrand Reinhold, 1971.

Sources of Needlepoint Supplies

United States

Boutique Margot, 26 West 54th
Street, New York, N. Y. 10019

The Haystack Ltd., 240 South
Beverly Drive, Beverly Hills, Calif.
90212

Iva Mae's Yarns, Heritage Village,
Southbury Conn. 06488

The Jewelled Needle, 920 Nicollet
Mall, Minneapolis, Minn. 55402

Krick Kits, 61 Portland Drive,
St. Louis, Mo. 63131

Virginia Maxell Studio, 3404 Kirby
Drive, Houston, Texas 77006

Alice Maynard, 558 Madison
Avenue, New York, N. Y. 10022

Needle Works, Ltd., 4035 Tulane
Avenue, New Orleans, La. 70119

The Needlecraft Shop, 4501 Van
Nuys Blvd., Sherman Oaks, Calif.
91403

The Needlepoint Works, 209 West
Eugenie, Chicago, Ill. 60614

Nimble Fingers, Inc., 283 Dartmouth
Street, Boston, Mass. 02116

The Purple Web, Pilgrim's Mall,
Woodbury, Conn. 06798

Selma's Art Needlework, 1645 Second
Avenue, New York, N. Y. 10028

The Stitchery, 204 Worcester
Turnpike, Wellesley Hills, Mass.
02181

Canada

Handcraft House, 110 West
Esplanade, North Vancouver,
B. C.

The Quest, 1150 Government St.,
Victoria, B. C.

Warwick Gallery Ltd., 2211 Granville
St., Vancouver, B. C.

Georgetown Hobbies & Craft, 28
Main N., Georgetown, Ontario

Needle and Thread, 361 Dundas St.,
London, Ontario

The Web, 160 Elgin St., Place Bell
Canada, Ottawa, Ontario

Condon's Yarns, P.O. Box 129,
Charlottetown, P.E.I.

Harmony Acres Studio, Bag 1550,
St. Norbert, Manitoba, R3V 1L4

Canadian Native Crafts, 250 Southern
Street, Vancouver, B. C.

Index of Stitches